£5.95

THE BEGINNER'S GUIDE TO
WOODWORKING

THE BEGINNER'S GUIDE TO
WOODWORKING

BLITZ EDITIONS

Copyright © RCS Rizzoli Libri 1995

Published by Blitz Editions
an imprint of Bookmart Ltd
Registered Number 2372865
Trading as Bookmart Ltd
Desford Road
Enderby
Leicester LE9 5AD

ISBN: 1 85605 284 2

Material previously published in 1992 as part of the
encyclopedia set *Be Creative (*Fabbri Publishing Ltd)

Editorial and design: Brown Packaging Ltd,
255-257 Liverpool Road, London N1 1LX

Printed in The Slovak Republic
51787

CONTENTS

STAR-STUDDED LETTER RACK

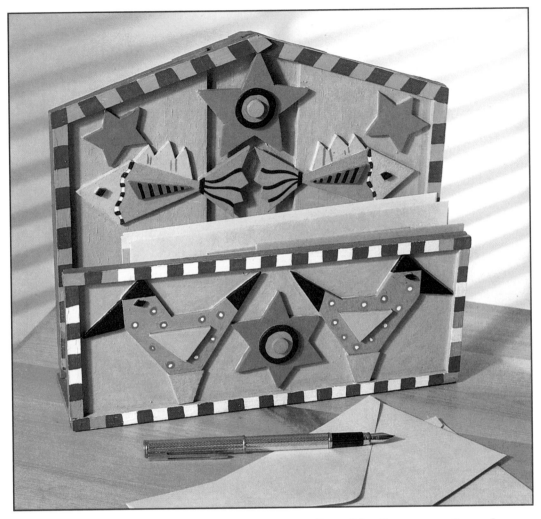

MATERIALS

For the letter rack shown *below left* you will need:

Above, three pieces of 5mm (³⁄₁₆) balsa; one length of 3mm (¹⁄₈) balsa; tube of balsa cement; craft knife; steel rule; cutting board; carbon paper; pencil.

Above, pot of acrylic gesso, or tube of white acrylic paint; polyurethane wood varnish; eight tubes of designers gouache, ultramarine, jet black, viridian lake, cool grey No 4, marigold yellow, warm grey No 2, permanent yellow deep, white; three paint brushes, sizes 1, 4 and 8; small palette; sheet of fine balsa sandpaper.

Our lively-looking letter rack is made of balsa wood and decorated with colourful balsa cut-outs. When you have become confident in the techniques used, you could make it in different colourways to blend with your own decor.

Balsa wood comes from a tropical American tree. It is the lightest of all commercial woods, with a very high strength for its weight, and is especially suitable for model making as it is very easy to cut and shape. It is sold in standard sizes of sheet, strip or block. For our letter rack only strip balsa is need, which can be bought from any good model shop. The various sections are glued with balsa cement — ordinary glue is not suitable.

Very few tools are required; the most essential item is a good craft knife, preferably the type with disposable blades and a safety lock. When working in balsa you will need to refit a new blade frequently to produce sharp, clean cuts. A blunt blade is unsatisfactory as the wood is more likely to splinter.

When all the cutting and gluing has been completed the whole letter rack is painted with gesso or white acrylic paint. This helps to fill in the grain and gives a smooth, uniform surface for applying the colours.

We have used designers gouache to decorate the letter rack. It is very similar to poster paint but generally of a higher quality. Art shops usually carry a large choice of colours, which is a great advantage as you may find colours that you did not know existed; this could inspire you to attempt your own exciting colour combinations.

The final step is to varnish the letter rack completely with matt clear varnish. This obviously makes it waterproof and gives a satisfactory matt finish that brings out the vibrancy of the colours.

HELPFUL HINT

Balsa wood is readily available from any good model or hobby shop.

When you become more confident working with balsa wood, you can construct your own letter rack decorated with your own motifs and to match your own colour scheme.

USING THE TEMPLATE

Enlarge the template on a photocopier to 150%. Place a piece of carbon paper (carbon side down) between your template and the piece of 3mm (⅛in) balsa and go over the birds, circles, fish and stars with a pencil. You may need to juggle the shapes around a little to make them fit on to the balsa.

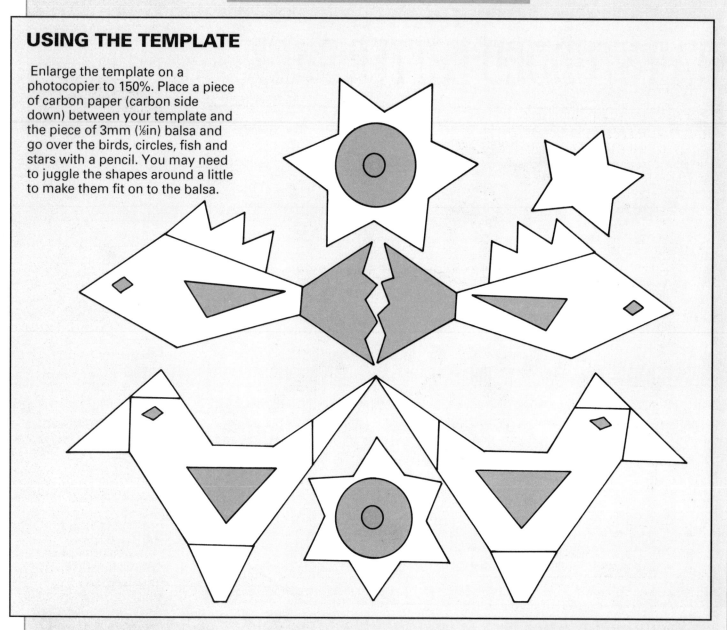

1 Use a craft knife to cut three 220 x 100mm (8¹⁄₁₆ x 4in) pieces of 5mm (³⁄₁₆in) balsa for the back of the rack. For the front, cut a piece of balsa 260 x 100mm (10¼ x 4in). Cut a piece 260 x 66mm (10¼ x 2⅝in) for the base.

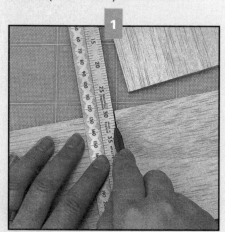

2 To make the back of the letter rack, draw a line 20mm (¾in) from the edge down both sides of one of your three pieces, as shown. Glue the three sections together with balsa cement, overlapping the two front pieces on either side of the middle piece and aligning the inner sides of the edge pieces with the pencil lines. Make certain the ends are level at the bottom. Use a generous amount of glue when working with balsa, particularly when you are gluing joints.

HELPFUL HINT

When cutting balsa, cut in straight lines, using a steel ruler as a guide. You will have to cut through the wood gently four or five times so that the piece you are cutting comes away cleanly.

3 Cut out the bird, fish, circle and star shapes. Sand the edges of all the pieces.

4 To shape the back of the rack, mark the centre (135mm (5⁵⁄₁₆in) from either side) of the middle piece. Then mark a point 40mm (1⁹⁄₁₆in) below the top of each side. Join your three points by drawing a diagonal line from the centre to each of the points at the sides. Cut along your guide lines.

5 Cut out the borders (see Cutting the Borders, *below right*) and sand each piece.

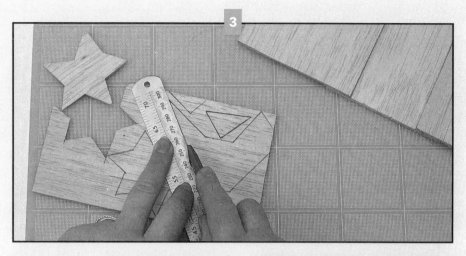

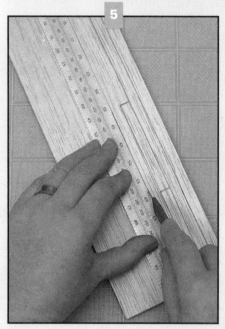

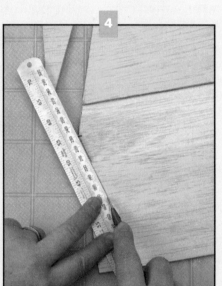

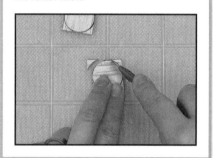

HELPFUL HINT

To cut the circles, draw a square around each one so that the sides of the square touch the circle at four points, as shown. Cut out the square, then carefully cut along each curve. You may need to practise this several times before cutting the circles for the letter rack.

CUTTING THE BORDERS

Using a pencil and a steel rule, mark out the strips for the borders on 5mm (³⁄₁₆in) balsa to the following sizes: two strips 265 x 7mm (10⁷⁄₁₆ x ¼in) and two strips 85 x 7mm (3⁵⁄₁₆ x ¼in) (these four pieces are used for the front); two strips 165 x 25mm (6½ x 1in) and two strips 140 x 25mm (5½ x 1in) (for the back).

6 Glue the borders to the back, angling the ends of the strips as shown where necessary, so that they fit snugly at the corners.

7 To cover the small gap in the top centre, cut out a small diamond, or a triangle, and glue it firmly in place.

8 Glue the two small stars and the bodies of the fish in place. Glue the circles to the large star. The large star in the centre and the two fish tails are supported on small blocks. To make the blocks,

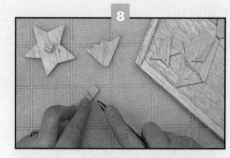

cut three 1-mm (¹⁄₃₂in) squares of 5mm (³⁄₁₆in) balsa and glue them on to the back of each piece. Glue the three pieces in place on to the centre section of the back.

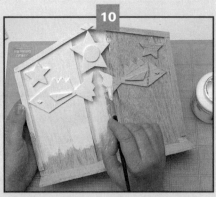

10 Use a large paint brush to apply the gesso to all sides of the letter rack. Make certain that you stir the gesso well — it should have the consistency of thick cream. Add water only if absolutely necessary. Leave to dry for about an hour. If the back bows slightly, place a weight on top of the back once the gesso is dry and leave for an hour or so.

9 Glue the birds and star to the front of the letter rack and then glue the base on to the back. Cut a strip of 5mm (³⁄₁₆in) balsa 10 x 240mm (½ x 9⁷⁄₁₆ in) and glue the strip to the join. Hold in place for 2-3 minutes until the glue has dried.

COLOUR GUIDE

KEY

UB — Blue (ultramarine)
G — Green (viridian lake)
DG — Dark Grey (cool grey No 4)
O — Orange (marigold yellow)
Y — Yellow (permanent yellow deep)
PG — Pale Green (viridian and white)
WG — Warm grey No 2
W — White

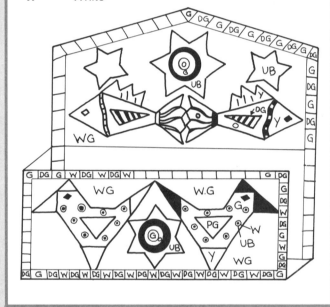

11 Paint the background with the warm grey and then paint the shapes, following the colour guide *above right*. Mix the colours with a little white paint to make the paint more opaque. Glue the front to the base and strengthen it on the inside with a strip of 5mm (³⁄₁₆in) balsa cut to 10 x 240mm (½ x 9⁷⁄₁₆ in). Paint the base and the reverse of the back. Paint the border and allow to dry for several hours.

12 Apply the varnish to all sides of the letter rack.

You can design your own cut-out decorations using flowers and leaves as a motif, or even simple house shapes to make a street scene. Sketch your ideas on paper first, then cut out the shapes and move them about until you are satisfied with the result. It is best to use the same number of cut-outs that we have used so that you don't obscure the lines of the letter rack.

CAT PENCIL BOX

This amusing pencil box is constructed from balsa wood, and develops the techniques that you have already learnt in the star-studded letter rack project. It will make a highly original, yet functional, addition to a desk or table top.

The pencil box is made from three different weights of balsa wood, which is sold in standard sheet sizes in most model shops. You will need a whole sheet of the 5mm (³/₁₆in) balsa wood, but you can use off-cuts of the other thicknesses (a 350mm (13³/₄in) length of the 3mm (¹/₈in) balsa wood, and a 200mm (8in) length of the 12mm (¹/₂in) balsa wood). The box and the decorative pieces are cut from fairly lightweight balsa wood which can be cut easily with a sharp craft knife. The head and tail are made from a heavier gauge wood, and should be cut with a junior fretsaw.

It is important to mark up and cut out the pieces for the box accurately. Check at all stages of working that the lid slides easily into the box, and when you have assembled the pieces, smooth all the edges with sandpaper. Sealing the wood with two coats of gesso will fill in the grain and provides a good surface to paint on; it will also help to strengthen the box. The varnish will darken the colours slightly, but will protect the paint from smudging and finger marks. The features, expression and decoration of the cat are highly stylised, and can be copied by using the templates provided. Alternatively, use your drawing skills to produce a more personal design.

If you want to use your own cat as a model, make a number of drawings from life or from photographs. Simplify the drawing of the head and the tail, exaggerating the expression of the face, or the curve of the tail, and stylise the markings of the fur into a bold, abstract pattern. Make your own templates from your drawings, and choose your own range of colours for the decoration.

Cutting the wood

Use a sharp craft knife, preferably one with disposable blades. Make several light cuts along the guideline rather than one strong one, or you will splinter the wood. When using the fretsaw, work from both ends of the guideline until the cut meets in the middle.

MATERIALS

For the cat pencil box shown *below left* you will need:

Above, one sheet each of balsa wood, 3mm (¹/₈in), 5mm (³/₁₆in) and 12mm (¹/₂in) thick; craft knife; tube of balsa cement; steel ruler; carbon paper; pencil; ballpoint pen; junior fretsaw; set square.

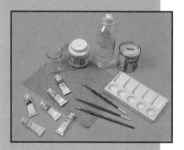

Above, acrylic gesso; sheet of fine balsa sandpaper; polyurethane clear matt wood varnish; palette; paintbrushes, sizes 4, 5 and 8; designer's gouache, cool grey no 4, warm grey no 2, black, white, mimosa yellow, geranium lake pale; white spirit.

HELPFUL HINT

A less decorative but more transportable version of this pencil box can be made by omitting the head and tail parts, and attaching small decorative brass hook and eyelets or another type of catch at each end of the box.

CAT FEATURES AND BOX DECORATION (Cut from **3mm (⅛in)** balsa wood)

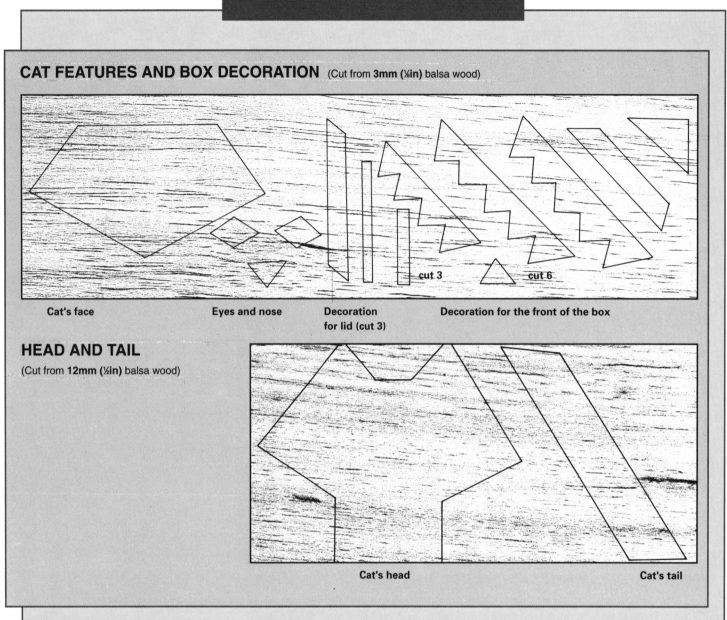

Cat's face   Eyes and nose   Decoration for lid (cut 3)   Decoration for the front of the box

cut 3   cut 6

HEAD AND TAIL
(Cut from **12mm (½in)** balsa wood)

Cat's head   Cat's tail

1 Use the measurements on the diagram to mark out the pieces for the main sections of the box on the 5mm (³/₁₆in) balsa wood using a ruler, set square and pencil. Make sure that the lines are straight and accurate. Go over the lines with a ballpoint pen if they are not very clear.

Cutting diagram for the box
(Cut from **5mm (³/₁₆in)** balsa wood)

(all measurements given are in mm: 25mm = 1in)

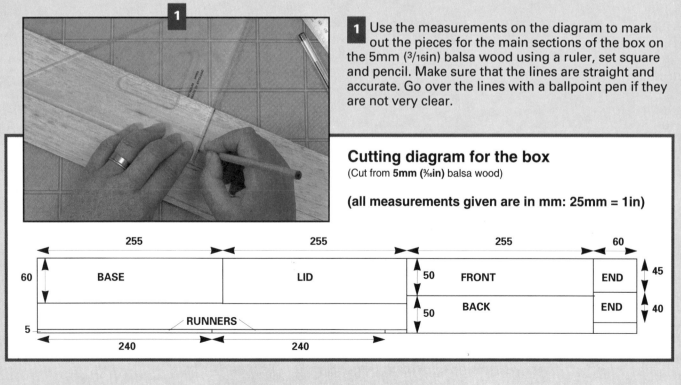

2 Cut out the main pieces of the box with a sharp craft knife, gradually cutting through the wood with several light strokes, rather than one strong cut.

3 Using balsa cement, glue the base between the front and back pieces, holding the box steady and square for a few minutes. Check that you can slide the lid in place easily. Leave to dry for about 10 minutes.

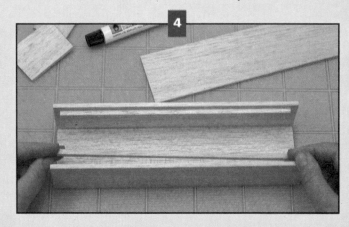

4 Measure 5mm (3/16in) — the thickness of the lid — from the top inside edges of the front and back of the box and mark with pencil. Glue the two runners in place, lining up the top with the pencil marks and making sure that they are straight. Again check that the lid will fit, and that it sits straight on the runners.

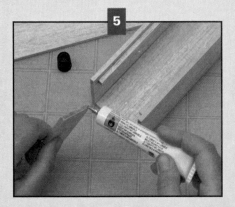

5 Glue both end pieces of the box in place.

6 Photocopy the template for the cat features & box decoration at 147%. Photocopy the head and tail template at 130% and transfer the design on to the 12mm (1/2in) balsa wood with carbon paper. Go over the lines with ballpoint pen, and cut out using a junior fretsaw.

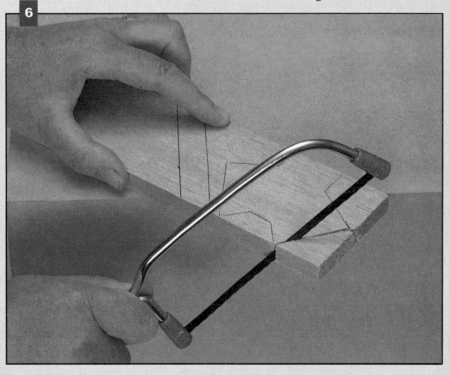

7 Cut a 5mm (³/₁₆in) strip off the end of the lid, so that it now measures 250mm (9⁷/₈in) in length. At one end make a mark at the midpoint of the width, 20mm (³/₄in) from the edge. Centre one end of the tail on this mark and draw carefully around the shape. Cut out the piece on the inside of the line in order to achieve a good fit. Mark and cut the hole for the head in the same way at the other end. Spread a generous amount of glue around the base of the head and slot the head into the hole, then glue in the tail. Hold both pieces firmly while they dry.

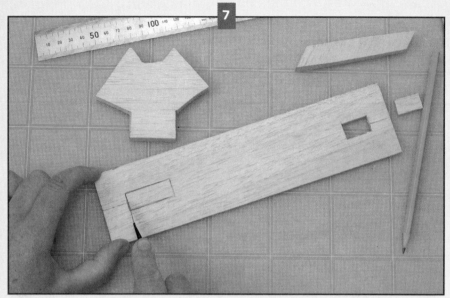

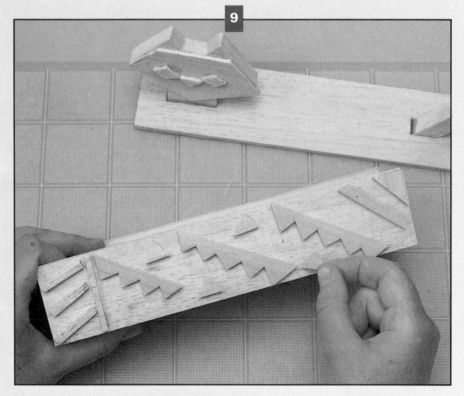

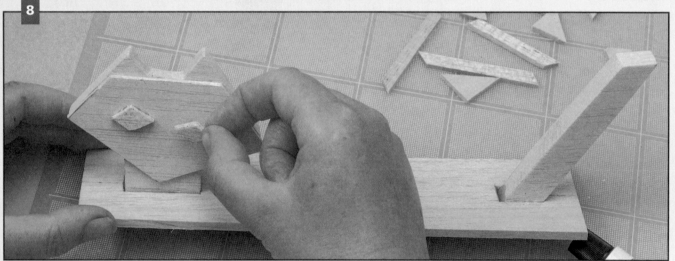

8 Transfer the design for the face, eyes and nose and decorative pieces on to the 3mm (¹/₈in) balsa wood and cut out with a sharp craft knife. Glue the face on to the head, then glue the eyes and nose on to the face. Leave to dry.

9 Glue the decorative pieces in place on the front of the box. Glue the 3 decorative pieces on to the lid. Leave to dry.

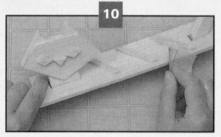

10 Carefully smooth the edges of the lid and the box with sandpaper.

COLOUR GUIDE

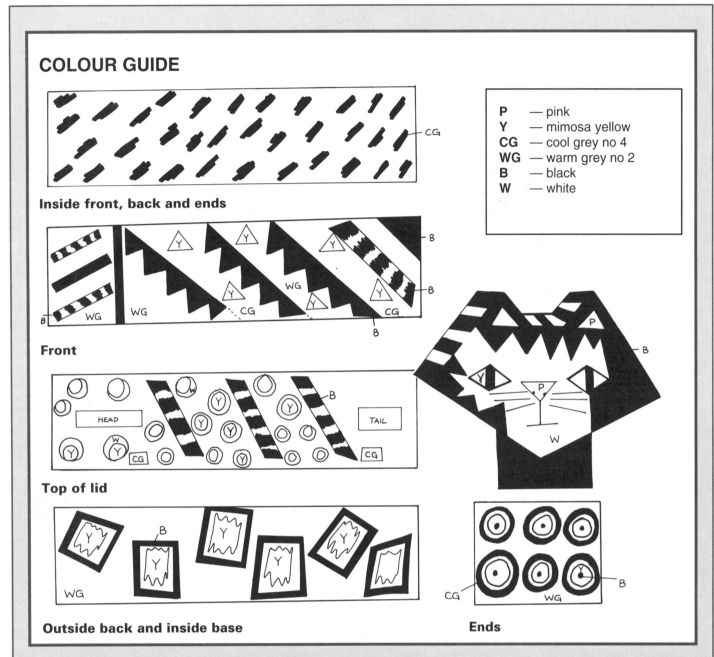

P	— pink
Y	— mimosa yellow
CG	— cool grey no 4
WG	— warm grey no 2
B	— black
W	— white

Inside front, back and ends

Front

Top of lid

Outside back and inside base

Ends

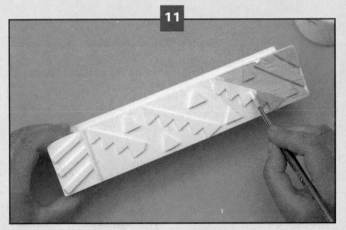

11 Use the largest brush to apply a coat of gesso over the whole box, inside and out. Leave to dry and apply a second coat. Leave to dry thoroughly for 24 hours. Wash the brush well with soap and water. Check that the lid fits; if it does not slide in easily, gently sand down and gesso the bare wood again.

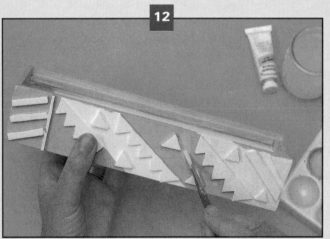

12 Paint the box following the colour guide (see box *above*). Paint warm grey no 2 over the entire surface of the inside of the lid and on the areas marked inside the box, then fill in the warm grey areas on the front, ends and back of the box.

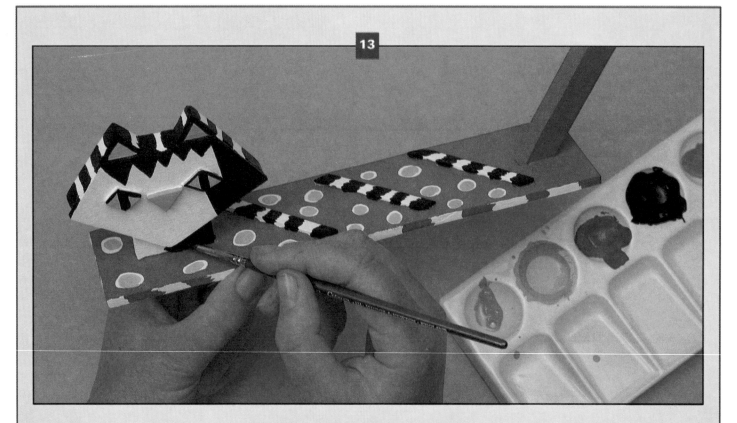

13 Paint all the cool grey no 4 areas, referring to the colour guide for the lid and the box; the inside of the front, back and ends are painted freehand. Leave to dry. Mix up pink by adding a touch of geranium lake pale to white, and paint the nose and ears. If the gesso is strong enough you will not need to paint the white areas. Paint the yellow areas, then the black areas — including the back of the head and the markings on the tail. Use the smallest paintbrush for the whiskers and mouth.

14 The back and the inside base of the box are painted with the same design. The squares, and the circles on the lid and ends of the box, are painted freehand, and you may want to practise them on paper first. Leave the paint to dry. Finally varnish the lid and the box and leave it to dry before assembling. Clean the brush with white spirit.

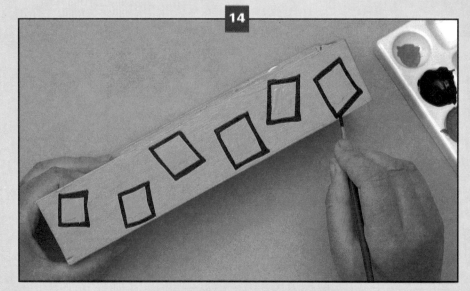

Using the same dimensions and construction for the box, you could make your own design for the head, tail and markings of another animal, or perhaps a bird, such as a duck or a peacock, using rich and vibrant colours.

SCULPTURE AND 3-D

SHIP MONEY BOX

Our colourful money box is made of balsa wood and painted with gouache paints. It incorporates an ingenious moving part designed to encourage the habit of thrift in young savers. A coin placed in the little model ship at the top of the incline propels the ship downwards, to deliver the money into the box through a slot at the bottom.

Children's money boxes with amusing devices to encourage saving were popular with the Victorians, and our money box is a modern interpretation of this idea. The box is constructed from balsa wood, and has a lift-up sliding door constructed in the same way as the sliding lid of our cat pencil box.

The moving part is worked by gravity. The weight of a coin placed in the ship at the top of the incline is enough to make it slide down the slope. When it reaches the bottom, the slot in the base of the ship meets the slot in the money box and the coin falls through. To get money out, it is a simple matter to slide up the door.

Acetate placed between the runners on the top of the box where the ship slides ensures that it has a smooth passage. Sheets of acetate can be bought at craft shops, but as such a tiny quantity is needed you may be able to find enough around the house on packaging for food and various household items.

The balsa wood is sold in sheets 10cm (4in) wide, and two weights are used, the lighter one for the decorative elements. As with the cat pencil box, some of the decoration is stuck on and some painted. We also introduce a new decorative technique — a small wooden block which is used to stamp the semi-circular wave motif.

MATERIALS

To make the money box shown *below left* you will need:

Above, sheet each of balsa wood 3mm (1/8in) and 6mm (1/4in) thick; craft knife; balsa cement; model filler; pencil; set square; black ballpoint pen; steel ruler; fine sandpaper; cutting board; acrylic gesso.

Above, designer's gouache paints: permanent green deep, zinc white, black, Naples yellow, Prussian blue, warm grey no 2; brushes size 1, 6 and 10; palette; water jar; sheet of acetate; all-purpose glue; gloss varnish; methylated spirits.

HELPFUL HINT

If the sliding mechanism of your ship tends to stick, take an old white candle, roll it in between your hands for a few minutes to soften the wax, and then rub the candle along the base of the ship.

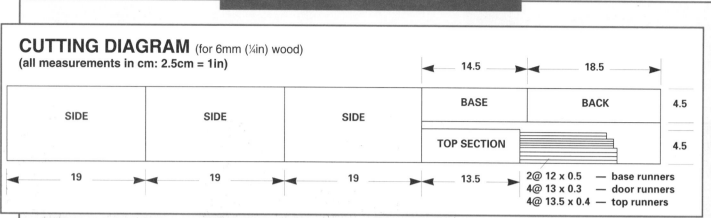

CUTTING DIAGRAM (for 6mm (¼in) wood)
(all measurements in cm: 2.5cm = 1in)

				14.5	18.5	
SIDE	SIDE	SIDE		BASE	BACK	4.5
				TOP SECTION		4.5
19	19	19	13.5			

2@ 12 x 0.5 — base runners
4@ 13 x 0.3 — door runners
4@ 13.5 x 0.4 — top runners

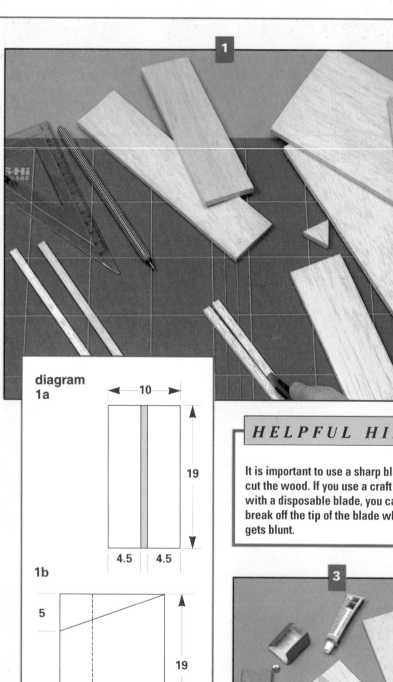

1 Following the diagram *above*, mark out the main sections for the money box on the 6mm balsa wood sheet. Cut out the sections with the craft knife using the ruler as a guide when cutting the large pieces.

2 On one of the side sections mark off longways strips 4.5cm (1³/₄in) wide (see diagram **1a**). Cut off these strips using the craft knife and ruler, and discard the shaded section. Glue one of these strips to each of the other two side sections with balsa cement, holding the pieces together until the cement sets. You now have two side sections each measuring 14.5 x 19cm (5³/₄ x 7¹/₂in). Leave to dry for 15 minutes.

diagram 1a

```
        10
   ┌──┬─┬──┐
   │  │ │  │
   │  │ │  │  19
   │  │ │  │
   └──┴─┴──┘
   4.5   4.5
```

1b

```
        ┌─────────┐
     5  │        ╱│
        │      ╱  │
        │    ╱    │  19
        │  ┊      │
        └──┴──────┘
       4.5   10
```

(all measurements in cm: 2.5cm = 1in)

HELPFUL HINT

It is important to use a sharp blade to cut the wood. If you use a craft knife with a disposable blade, you can break off the tip of the blade when it gets blunt.

3 Make a sanding block from off-cut balsa wood with a piece of sandpaper wrapped round it and held in position with a drawing pin. Fill the joins in the side sections with model filler, pressing it in firmly. Leave to dry for 15 minutes before sanding over the entire surface with the sanding block.

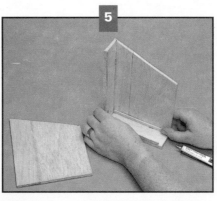

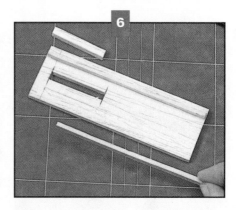

4 Mark the line of the incline on each side section (see diagram **1b**), using the ruler and ballpoint pen. Cut off the corner with the craft knife.

5 Glue the back piece to the upper surface of the base piece with balsa cement. Glue the base runners to the upper surface of the base, one lining up with each long edge. Glue the two side sections to the back and the base and hold in position while the balsa cement sets.

6 Mark and cut out the slot in the top section, and glue the top runners for the boat in position 2.5cm (1in) apart (see diagram **2**). Mark a line 2cm (³/₄in) from the top on the inside of each side section. Glue a top runner beneath each line. Cut the top end of the top section at an angle so that it fits to the back, and glue in place.

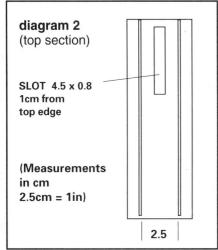

diagram 2
(top section)

SLOT 4.5 x 0.8
1cm from
top edge

(Measurements in cm
2.5cm = 1in)

2.5

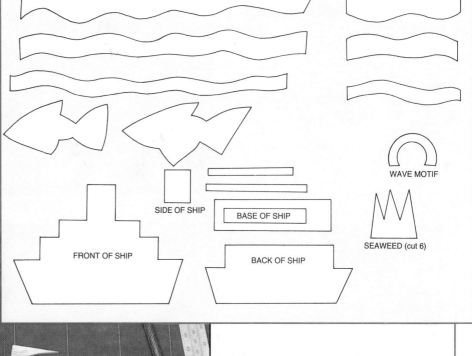

DECORATION TEMPLATE (for 3mm (⅛in) wood)

WAVE MOTIF

SEAWEED (cut 6)

SIDE OF SHIP

BASE OF SHIP

FRONT OF SHIP

BACK OF SHIP

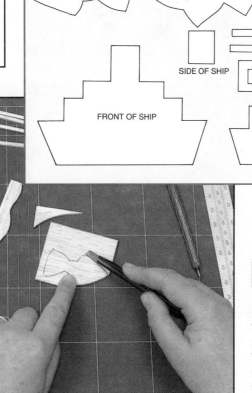

7 Cut a piece for the door measuring 13 x 4.3cm (5¹/₈ x 1¹¹/₁₆in) from the 3mm (¹/₈in) thick balsa wood. Enlarge the template for the decorative pieces on a photocopier to 200%. Transfer to the 3mm (¹/₈in) balsa sheet and cut out all the shapes (except the semi-circular wave motif) with the craft knife. Use the sanding block to sand over all surfaces.

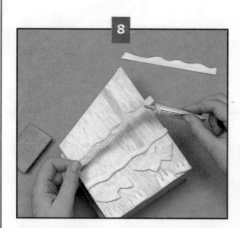

8 Glue the decorative pieces to the back and one side of the box following diagram **3**, *below*.

diagram 3

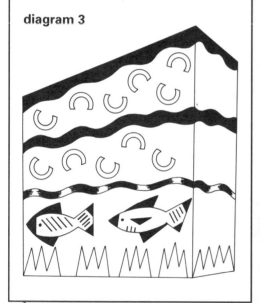

9 Cut a triangular piece of 6mm (¹/₄in) balsa (each side 2cm/ ³/₄in) and glue to the door. Glue on the two sets of door runners. Glue the rear ones inside the box on the side sections 10cm (4in) away from the front edge. Glue the front runners flush with the front edge of the side sections. Ensure that there is at least 3.5mm (¹/₈in) between the two runners and check that the door slides up and down easily.

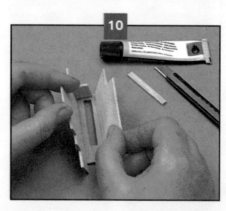

10 Cut out the slot from the base piece of the ship (see Decoration template on previous page). To assemble the ship, glue the small end piece to the front of the base piece, and then glue the front and back pieces in position. Glue the decorative strips to the front piece.

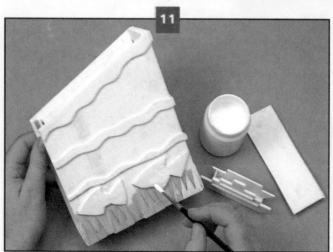

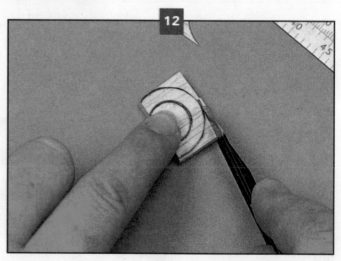

11 With the size 6 brush, paint the box, the door and the ship with the gesso. Leave to dry.

12 Using the craft knife cut a 3 x 2cm (1³/₁₆ x ³/₄in) rectangle for a printing block from a scrap of 6mm (¹/₄in) balsa. Trace the semi-circular wave motif on to the balsa. With the craft knife, cut round the motif, pressing the knife in to 2mm (¹/₁₆in) depth. Trim away the wood from the remainder of the block surface, leaving a raised semi-circle.

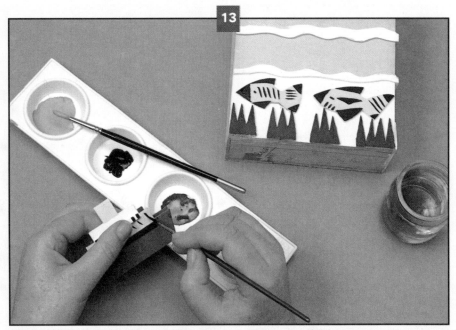

13 Mix Prussian blue with white gouache to make a pale blue and with the size 6 brush, paint the top, undecorated side and door of the box. Paint the decorated side and back with the same colour except for the bottom sections. Add white to the mix to make a paler blue and paint these sections. Paint the fish, seaweed and ship following the colour guide *below*, using the size 1 brush for the fine black details.

COLOUR GUIDE

B	black		**VPB**	very pale blue	} all Prussian Blue
Y	Naples yellow		**LB**	light blue	with varying
W	zinc white		**MB**	mid blue	amounts of white
G	warm grey no. 2		**DKB**	dark blue	
DG	permanent green deep				

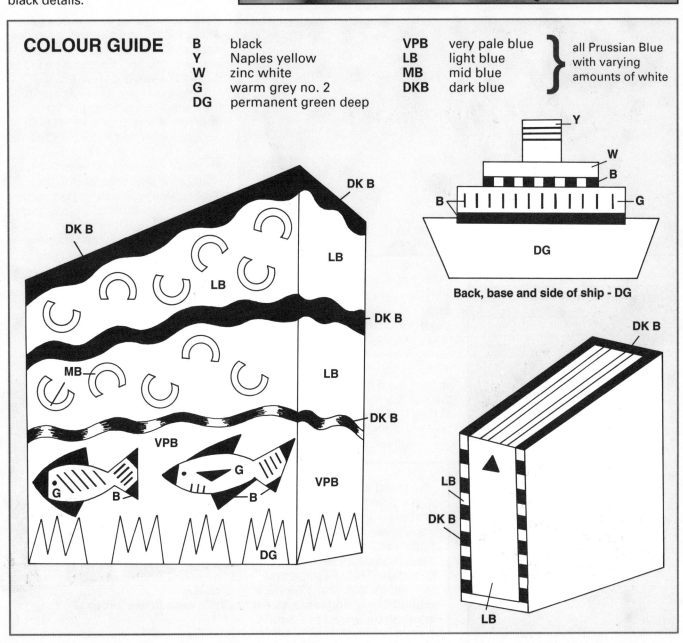

Back, base and side of ship - DG

14 Using the size 6 brush and a medium mix of Prussian blue and white, cover the printing block thickly with paint and print the wave motif on to the two top sections of the decorated side and back of the box. Re-load the block frequently with paint and turn it in all directions to make a random pattern.

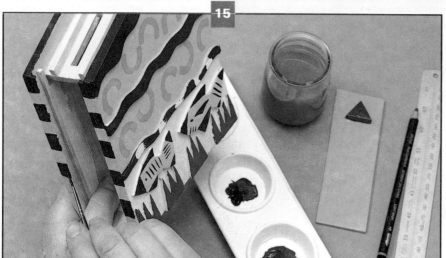

15 Mix Prussian blue with a tiny quantity of white and paint the door knob and all round the top edges of the box. Paint the raised decorative wave pieces, leaving white gaps at five intervals along the lowest wave. Measure 1cm intervals down both sides of the door opening and mark with the pencil. Starting at the top, paint alternate 1cm squares with Prussian blue. Leave to dry. Clean the brushes with methylated spirit.

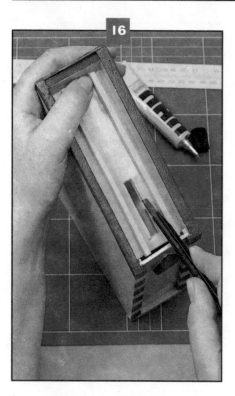

16 Measure a piece 135 x 22mm (5⁵/₁₆ x ⁷/₈in) on the acetate sheet and mark by scratching with the craft knife. Cut with the knife and glue with all-purpose glue on to the top of the box. Use the craft knife to cut out the acetate over the slot. Varnish all the surfaces of the box and ship and leave to dry overnight. Clean the brush with methylated spirits.

You could use the basic idea of our money box to produce a box with a completely different theme. A car, lorry or perhaps aeroplane could be substituted for the boat, and the underwater scene on the box could be replaced by a landscape, street scene or aerodrome with appropriate decorative motifs.

SCULPTURE AND 3-D

MUSICAL BOX

MATERIALS

To make the musical box shown *below left* you will need:

Above, 3 sheets of balsa wood, 3mm, 5mm and 6mm (1/8in, 3/16in & 1/4in) thick; length of 1cm (3/8in) dowelling; conversion kit for mobiles; craft knife; compasses; balsa cement; steel ruler; pencil; black ballpoint pen; set square; pair of metal snips; bradawl; cutting mat.

Above, designer's gouache paints: viridian lake, cobalt pale hue, lemon yellow, brilliant yellow, cool grey no. 2, scarlet lake, white, black; brushes size 1, 4 and 8; palette; water jar; fine and medium grade sandpaper; 20mm (3/4in) decorator's brush; gesso; matt varnish; white spirit.

Our balsa wood musical box is based on the theme of a ballet dancer on a stage — as the music plays a hidden mechanism makes the dancing figure revolve. Gaily painted in naive style, it will appeal to adults and children alike.

The first musical box was invented by a Swiss watchmaker in 1796, but it was the early American settlers who began to make musical boxes which incorporated moving figures, or automatons. Examples of these in museums can still provide amusement today.

The mechanism for our musical box, which provides the music and propels the dancer, is adapted from a standard conversion kit designed to turn an ordinary child's mobile into a musical mobile. The mechanism is housed 'below stage' and the winding handle is positioned at the back. When constructing the musical box it is important to ensure that the revolving metal pin of the mechanism, on which the dancer sits, is positioned vertically. Also the hole in

the stage floor must be centred above the pin so that the dancer can turn with ease. As with earlier balsa wood projects, some of the decoration is glued on and some painted.

The dancer is made from two cut-out shapes glued either side of a flattened piece of dowel; the shapes should be painted on both sides, inside and out, because these will be visible as the dancer turns. There are a number of small, intricate shapes to cut out so you will need to use a sharp blade at all times to produce clean cuts.

When the musical box is completed it is sanded with medium and then fine grade sandpaper and given a coat of gesso. This gives an even surface for applying the colours, and produces a professional finish.

Cut from 6mm (¹/₄in) wood (all measurements in mm: 25mm = 1in)

SIDE WEDGES

| BOX SIDE | BOX SIDE | BOXBASE | BACK CASING | FRONT CASING |

100 · 95

220 · 220 · 117 · 6 · 117 · 117

Cut from 5mm (³/₁₆in) wood

130 · 120 · 130 · 134

| BOX FRONT | CURTAINS | | STAGE BACK |

SCRAP WOOD:
wedges can be cut out of these pieces

100

33 · 20 · 35 · back · 30 · front · 15

DECORATIVE EDGE (TOP)

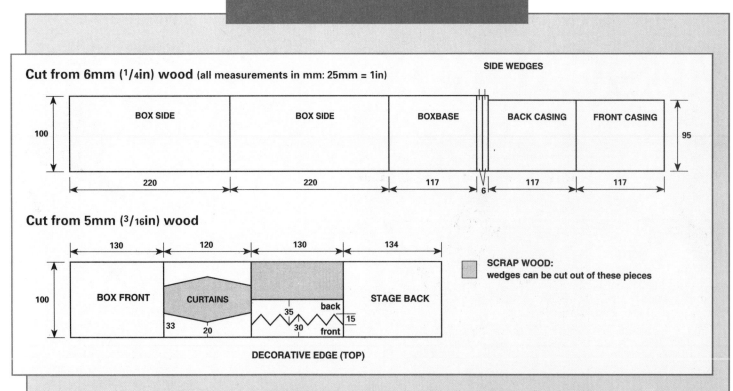

1 Following the diagram *above*, mark out the main sections for the musical box on the 5mm (³/₁₆in) and 6mm (¹/₄in) balsa wood. Cut out the sections with the craft knife, using the set square as a guide to keep the angles straight.

2 Glue the box sides to the outside edges of the box base with balsa cement, holding the pieces together until the cement sets. Leave to dry for 15 minutes, then glue the box front in place in the same way.

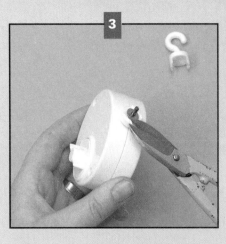

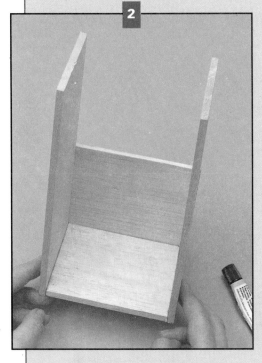

3 Cut off the plastic hook on the musical conversion kit using metal cutters or tin snips. This exposes the metal pin on which the dancer will be placed.

4 To make the casing for the musical mechanism, make a pencil mark halfway along the long edge of the back casing, 35mm (1³/₈in) from the edge. With the compass point on this mark, draw a circle 35mm (1³/₈in) in diameter. Carefully cut out the circle with the craft knife and smooth the edges with a small piece of sandpaper.

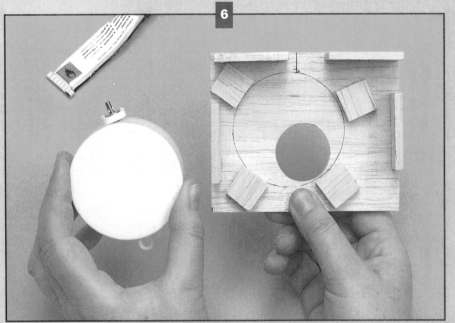

5 Place the musical mechanism in position, with the winding handle jutting through the hole and the metal pin centred vertically. Draw around the mechanism with a ballpoint pen and mark the position of the pin.

6 Cut four 20 x 20mm (³/₄ x ³/₄in) squares from 5mm (³/₁₆in) balsa and glue them flush with the mechanism to hold it in place. Cut four 28 x 45mm (1¹/₈ x 1³/₄in) pieces from 5mm (³/₁₆in) balsa; glue two of them to the top edge, either side of the pin, and one on either side as shown. Leave to dry.

7 Put the mechanism in place, then glue on the front casing. Draw a line 34mm (1³/₈in) from the edge of the box base. Slide the casing into position, lining it up with the pencil line and with the winding handle facing outwards. Glue in place.

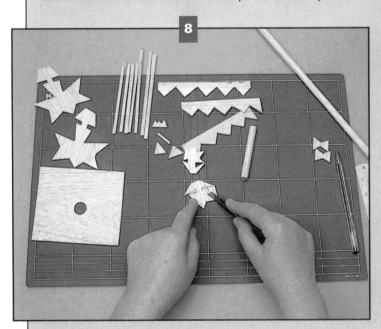

8 Cut a piece for the stage floor measuring 100 x 117mm (4 x 4⁵/₈in) from the 3mm (¹/₈in) thick balsa wood. Slide it into place and press it on to the metal pin so that it makes an indent in the wood. Using this mark as the centre, cut out an 18mm (³/₄in) diameter hole in the wood. Enlarge the decoration template on a photocopier to 176%. Transfer to the 3mm (¹/₈in) balsa sheet and cut out the shapes with the craft knife. Use fine sandpaper to smooth all the edges. Cut a 70mm (2³/₄in) length of dowel for the dancer's leg.

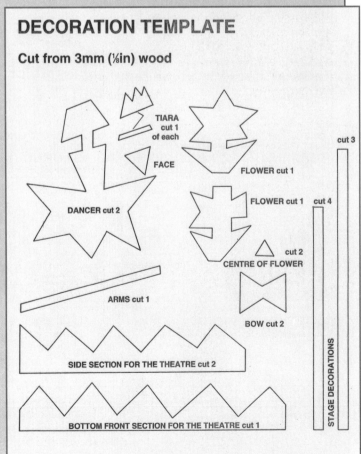

DECORATION TEMPLATE

Cut from 3mm (¹/₈in) wood

TIARA cut 1 of each

FACE

FLOWER cut 1

DANCER cut 2

FLOWER cut 1

cut 3

cut 4

CENTRE OF FLOWER cut 2

ARMS cut 1

BOW cut 2

SIDE SECTION FOR THE THEATRE cut 2

BOTTOM FRONT SECTION FOR THE THEATRE cut 1

STAGE DECORATIONS

9 Assemble the front of the dancer by gluing the face and tiara pieces in position, and the arm piece at an angle across the back of the shoulders. Place the point of the dancer's dress 35mm (1³/₈in) from the end of the dowelling leg. Draw around the dowelling at this point and then carve away the dowel from there to the end to flatten it. Repeat on the other side. This makes it easier to glue the dancer to the dowel later on.

10 Glue the centre triangles to the flowers. Glue the bows to the curtains. Glue the 5 x 5mm (³/₁₆ x ³/₁₆in) wedges to the base of the flowers at the back. With the point of the bradawl make a hole 12mm (¹/₂in) deep in the base of the leg so it will fit on the metal pin.

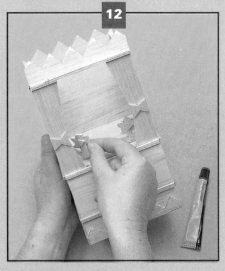

11 Glue the curtains to the front of the box. Glue the zig-zag decorative pieces in place at the top, bottom and sides, then add the straight decorative strips. Check that the corners are neat.

12 Glue the stage floor in position, then the stage back and the zig-zag top. Glue the 100 x 6mm (4 x ¹/₄in) side wedges along the tops of the side pieces to give a neat finish. Glue the flowers in place on the stage floor, one slightly in front of the other. Allow time for the glue to dry.

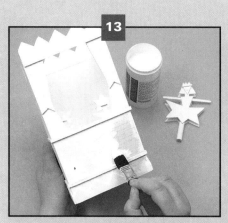

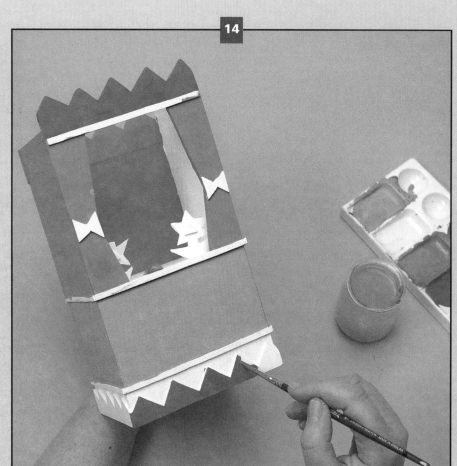

13 Lightly sand the box to give a smooth finish, then apply a coat of gesso over the whole box and the dancer with the 3/4-inch decorator's brush. Leave to dry.

14 Mix pastel blue from cobalt blue and white and, using the size 8 brush, paint the outside of the upper stage, the curtains and the inside back of the stage. Mix cobalt with less white to make a darker blue and paint the zig-zag trims at top and base with the size 4 brush. Mix viridian lake and white. Paint the central section of the box.

COLOUR GUIDE

G	green	**FP**	flesh pink
PG	pale green	**LY**	light yellow
B	blue	**BY**	bright yellow
BP	bright pink	**BL**	black
PP	pale pink	**CG**	cool grey
		PB	pale blue

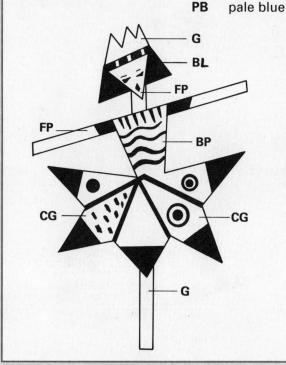

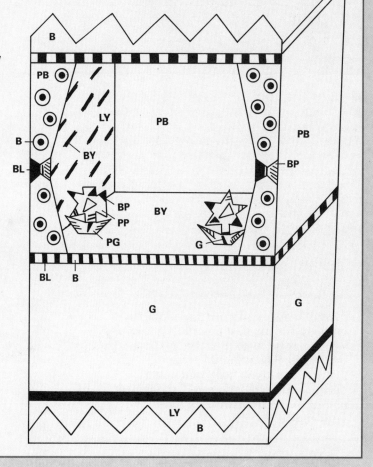

15 Paint the decorative elements following the colour guide on the previous page, using the size 1 brush for the smaller details. Paint the two shapes for the dancer (remembering to paint both back and front of each piece) and the dowel leg, following the colour guide. Leave to dry, then glue the dancer shapes to the flat sections of the dowel. Using the 3/4-inch decorator's brush, apply a coat of matt varnish to the music box and the dancer. Leave to dry.

Fit the dancer on to the metal pin, then wind up the musical box mechanism and watch her perform graceful pirouettes to the music. Following the basic instructions given here, you could design your own 'stage set' and dancer and decorate them in the colours of your choice.

SCULPTURE AND 3-D

JEWELLERY BOX

MATERIALS

To make the jewellery box shown *below left* you will need:

Above, 2 sheets of 6mm (¼in) balsa wood; 2 sheets 0.8mm (¹⁄₃₂in) balsa wood; short length of 1cm (³⁄₈in) dowel; 2 brass hinges, 20mm (¾in), plus screws; 2 sheets of sandpaper, medium and fine grade; 2 sanding blocks made from scrap balsa and fine and medium grade sandpaper; craft knife; cutting mat; steel ruler; ballpoint pen; small screwdriver; pins; compasses; acrylic gesso or medium; 20mm (¾in) decorator's brush; balsa glue; balsa wood filler.

Above, black self-stick felt, about 46 x 28cm (18 x 11in); brass box catch, 32 x 20mm (1¼ x ¾in); small hammer; scissors; gloss varnish; methylated spirits; gouache paints: carmine, black, gold and white; palette; round watercolour brushes, sizes 1, 2, and 5.

Continuing our series of decorative and practical balsa wood boxes, we show you in this project how to construct a felt-lined jewellery box with a hinged lid and a drawer.

I f you have been following our projects in balsa wood, you will by now be familiar with the basic techniques used to make boxes. The jewellery box we are making in this project is lined with felt, and we also show you how to make a drawer, and how to hinge the lid of the box and close it with a clasp. The brass hinges and screws used are very small, so you will probably need an electric screwdriver to fix them.

The relief decoration on the box is made from almost paper-thin balsa wood. This needs to be cut out very carefully, particularly when cutting across the grain. The edges of each shape are gently smoothed with sandpaper, which is also a delicate job, but necessary to give the box a good finish. The colour is applied with gouache paints, and the box is then given a coat of gloss varnish to make it shine.

HELPFUL HINT

Instead of using a piece of dowel for the bottom drawer, you could buy a small brass or wooden handle. Screw the handle through the drawer and fix it with a washer and nut.

CUTTING DIAGRAM (all measurements in mm: 25mm = 1in)

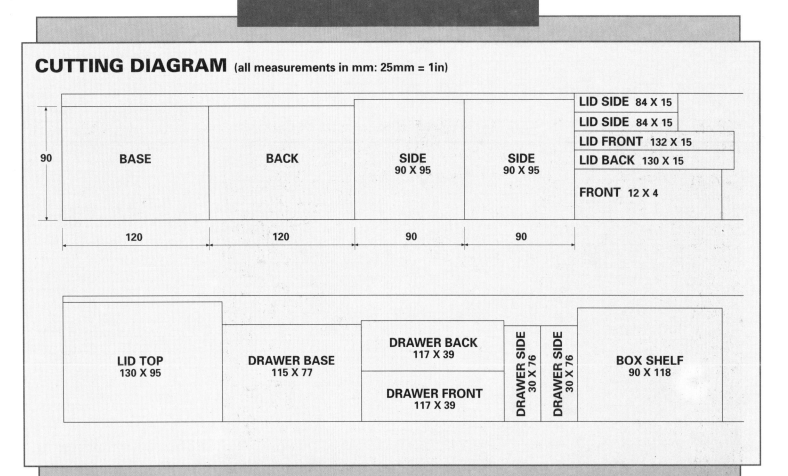

90	BASE	BACK	SIDE 90 X 95	SIDE 90 X 95	LID SIDE 84 X 15
					LID SIDE 84 X 15
					LID FRONT 132 X 15
					LID BACK 130 X 15
					FRONT 12 X 4
	120	120	90	90	

LID TOP 130 X 95	DRAWER BASE 115 X 77	DRAWER BACK 117 X 39	DRAWER SIDE 30 X 76	DRAWER SIDE 30 X 76	BOX SHELF 90 X 118
		DRAWER FRONT 117 X 39			

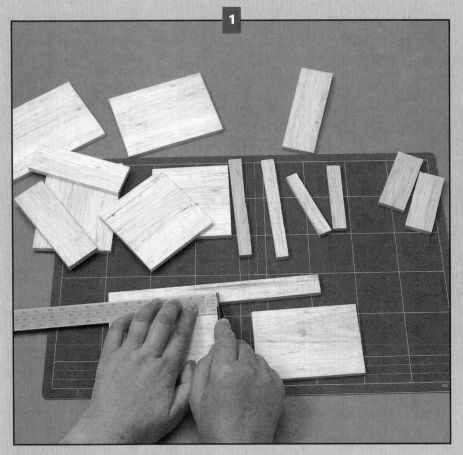

1 Mark out the pieces for the main sections of the jewellery box on the two pieces of 6mm (1/4in) balsa wood following the diagram *above*. Go over the lines with a ballpoint pen if they are not very clear. Cut out the sections with a craft knife and steel ruler.

2 Using balsa cement, glue the back and side sections to the edges of the base to make the casing. Insert a few pins through the wood at the corners and maintain light pressure with the fingers for a few minutes to hold the casing steady and square. Leave to dry for about 10 minutes.

3 Assemble and glue the drawer section, gluing the front to the base, then the back and the sides. Leave to dry. Slide the drawer into the bottom of the casing, then slide the box shelf on top of the drawer, leaving a 1mm ($^1/_{32}$in) gap between them. Hold in place while you mark the position with a pen line, then remove the drawer and glue the shelf in place. Leave to dry.

4 Glue the front of the casing in place. Assemble and glue the lid of the box, first gluing the front and back to the top, then sliding the sides in between them (sand the edges of the pieces if necessary to get a good fit). Pin at the corners and leave to dry.

HELPFUL HINT

Any gaps between joins can be filled with balsa wood filler. Don't worry if there is a gap around the drawer front — when the wood is gessoed and painted it will be slightly thicker.

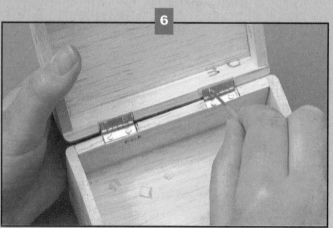

5 Remove the pins. Smooth off the box and lid using the two sanding blocks, first the medium grade and then the fine grade. Use the sanding blocks also to round off all the corners on both box and lid.

6 Lay the brass hinges along the top edge of the casing (at the back), about 2cm ($^3/_4$in) from the corners. Mark their positions on the wood. Using a craft knife, carefully cut down into the wood to a depth of about 1mm ($^1/_{32}$in) where the hinges are to go. Screw the hinges to the back of the box. Repeat for the box lid and screw the hinges in place as shown. Check that everything fits neatly and the lid closes tightly — if not, shave away more wood beneath the hinge flaps.

7 Photocopy the template for the decorative pieces at 133% and transfer the outlines to the 0.8mm (¹/₃₂in) balsa wood with carbon paper. Go over the lines with ballpoint pen, and cut out using a craft knife with a very sharp blade. As the wood is very thin it tends to split easily, so patience is needed! Cut a 1cm (⅜in) length of dowel to make the handle for the drawer.

8 Sand all the decorative pieces carefully with fine grade sandpaper to round off the edges. Glue the pieces in place, following the colour guide diagram, *right.* Using the balsa cement, glue the handle to the drawer front.

THE DECORATIVE PIECES

x2

x2

x2

x2

x3

x2

x2

x3

x4

x2

x4

x3

COLOUR GUIDE

The sides and back are painted red with no decoration

9 Smooth the whole box and the drawer using fine grade sandpaper, then use a decorator's brush to apply a coat of gesso over the box and drawer, except for the insides of the drawer, the upper tray and the box lid. Leave to dry.

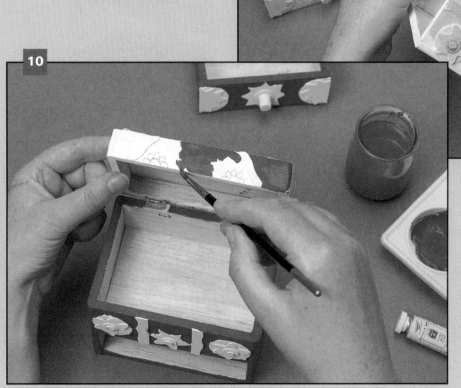

10 To paint the box, follow the colour guide *above*. First squeeze about 5cm (2in) of carmine paint on to the palette and mix with a little white. Paint the box and drawer using the size 5 brush, working around the decorative shapes. Leave to dry.

11 Use the size 1 and 3 brushes to paint all the gold and black areas, referring to the colour guide. Leave to dry thoroughly, then varnish all the painted areas with gloss varnish.

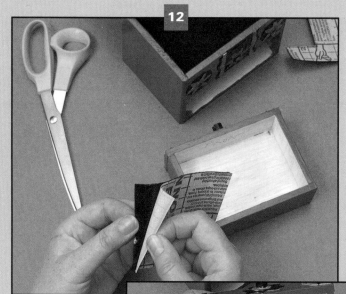

CUTTING GUIDE FOR FELT LINING

Drawer
base   10 x 7.5cm (4 x 3in)
sides   35 x 3.3cm (13¾ x 1¼in)

Inside lid
base   12 x 8.2cm (4¾ x 3¼in)
sides   40.4 x 1.4cm (15⅞ x ⁹⁄₁₆in)

Upper tray
base   12 x 8.2cm (4¾ x 3¼in)
sides   40.4 x 3.7cm (15⅞ x 1½in)

12 When the varnish is dry, measure and cut out the black felt pieces for lining the drawer, upper tray and inside of the lid, using the cutting guide *left*. The side linings are cut in one long piece. To fit the pieces, first peel away a corner of the backing sheet, then gradually peel off the rest of the backing sheet as you press the felt in place.

13 Close the lid and position the brass clasp on the front of the box, making sure it is centred. Use a small hammer to tap the tiny pins into the wood.

Using this project as a guide, you could construct your own 'treasure chest' with several drawers, decorated with your own motifs and to your own colour scheme.

SCULPTURE AND 3-D

VASE IN WOOD

MATERIALS

To make the vase, leaves and flowers shown *below left* you will need:

Above, cutting board; carbon paper; fine sand paper; steel ruler; pencil; craft knife; masking tape; coping saw; wood glue.

Above, vice; small hammer; drill with wood bits in the following sizes, $1/16$, $1/8$, $1/4$; 3mm ($1/8$in) chisel.

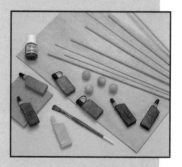

Above, small offcut of $3/4$in MDF (medium density fibreboard) at least 100 x 100mm (4 x 4in); one piece of $3/4$in balsa, 500 x 300 mm ($19^3/4$ x $11^3/4$in), with the grain running lengthwise; dowel (ramin) in the following sizes — three 900mm ($35^1/2$in) lengths, $1/8$in thick; four 900mm ($35^1/2$in) lengths, $1/4$in thick; one 900mm ($35^1/2$in) length, $5/16$in thick; four 25mm (1in) wooden balls; Rotring or Staedtler waterproof drawing inks in: green, purple, blue, yellow, red and black; Pelikan waterproof drawing ink in carmine; 25mm (1in) nylon brush.

This is the first of two projects on creating an appealing zany sculpture from wood. Here we show you how to make the wooden vase to hold the highly stylised colourful leaves and flowers that are the subject of another project.

This two-part lesson is an introduction to the idea of using everyday materials in a slightly unexpected way. Using plywood and dowel, we show you how to construct an unusual but fascinating wooden sculpture. The 'base' of the sculpture is an asymmetrical vase, which supports the other elements of the design — the leaves and flowers.

You can use your own creative imagination to determine the appearance of the finished object by varying the colours, the shapes of the leaves and the arrangement of the flowers and leaves in the vase. If you wish, you can use the vase to hold natural objects — dried teasels and/or other dried seed heads would look attractive — and you could also paint the vase in complementary colours. However, don't use the vase for fresh flowers or leaves as it is not watertight.

Materials and construction

With the exception of the few materials that are needed to mould the dowel for the stems, on this page we have listed all the materials you will need for the two lessons. The plywood and dowel are available from timber merchants and the wooden balls from model-making shops.

You should allow at least three days to complete the vase; although the techniques are simple and easy to follow, you must allow time for the glue to dry (at least overnight) at two different stages during construction.

THE TEMPLATES

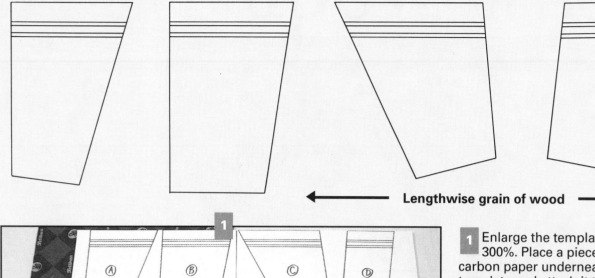

Lengthwise grain of wood

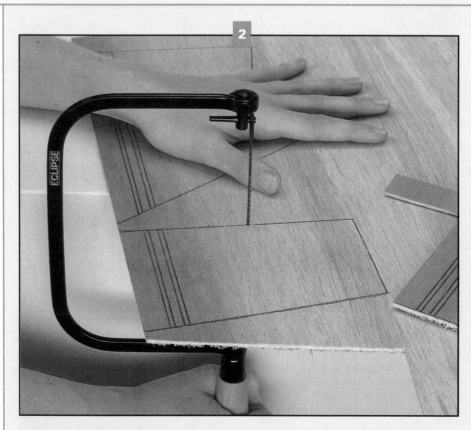

1 Enlarge the template to 300%. Place a piece of carbon paper underneath the template and attach it to the board with masking tape, making certain that the grain of the wood runs in the direction of the arrow. Go over the design with a pencil. (Depending on the size of your carbon and photocopy paper, you may have to trace shapes A and B first and then trace shapes C and D.)

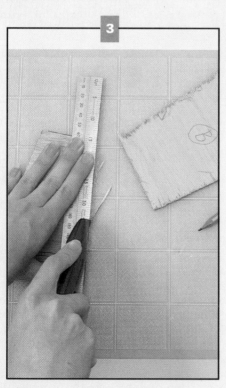

2 Cut out the shapes with the coping saw, keeping the lines as straight as you can. Turn the blade of the saw to cut around the edges. Don't cut into the space between B and C; you will need this and the remaining pieces of the plywood for the leaves.

3 If you have not already done so, label each piece on the back. Straighten the edges of the pieces with a craft knife; they must be cut as accurately as possible or the vase will not fit together.

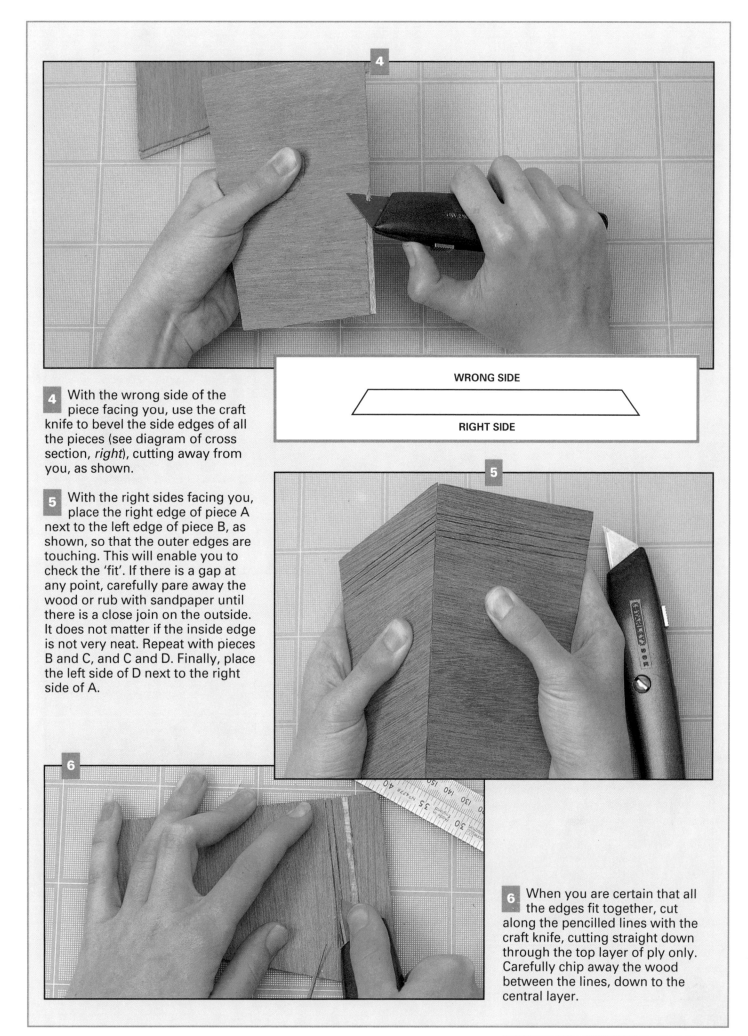

WRONG SIDE

RIGHT SIDE

4 With the wrong side of the piece facing you, use the craft knife to bevel the side edges of all the pieces (see diagram of cross section, *right*), cutting away from you, as shown.

5 With the right sides facing you, place the right edge of piece A next to the left edge of piece B, as shown, so that the outer edges are touching. This will enable you to check the 'fit'. If there is a gap at any point, carefully pare away the wood or rub with sandpaper until there is a close join on the outside. It does not matter if the inside edge is not very neat. Repeat with pieces B and C, and C and D. Finally, place the left side of D next to the right side of A.

6 When you are certain that all the edges fit together, cut along the pencilled lines with the craft knife, cutting straight down through the top layer of ply only. Carefully chip away the wood between the lines, down to the central layer.

7 Lay pieces A and B face down and side by side on your work surface so that they are as close together as as you can get them. Stick a piece of masking tape down the join. Repeat with the edges of pieces B and C, C and D and finish with pieces D and A. Fold the box loosely together. If two edges do not fit closely together, remove the masking tape and pare away some more wood to correct the angle of the join. Re-stick to check the fit.

8 When you are satisfied with the corner joins, remove the masking tape from one of the corners and lay the pieces flat on your work surface. Squeeze plenty of glue down each join and along the outside edges. It does not matter too much it is is a bit messy, although you could wipe off the worst lumps with a damp cloth.

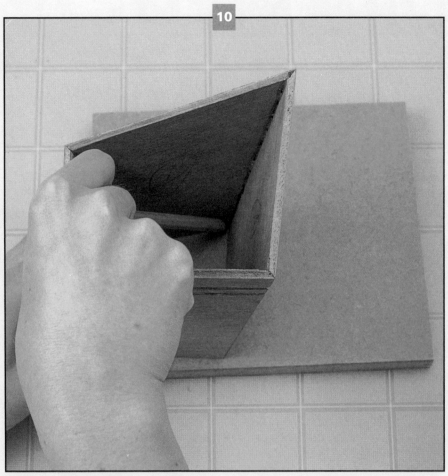

9 Fold the vase up again and secure the final join with tape. Leave it to dry overnight (longer if possible) in a warm, dry place.

10 Remove the masking tape carefully and stand the vase on the composition board. Using a long pencil, and working from the inside of the vase, draw the shape of the base of the vase on to the board. Mark a cross in one corner of both the base and the vase, so that you can fit the base accurately later on.

11 Cut out the base with the coping saw and test it for size by dropping it into the vase, matching the crosses at the corners. Don't force it; it should drop in easily, leaving a gap where the vase slopes away from the bottom. If the fit is too tight, pare the edges of the base to reduce it a little in size.

12 Stick masking tape around the bottom edge and, again working from the inside, squeeze lots of glue into the gap. Leave to dry as before for about 12 to 16 hours, as the glue is extremely thick.

13 When the glue seems thoroughly dry, sand the outside and edges of the vase gently. Mix a very dark blue colour with 50% black, 50% blue ink. You should mix plenty as the wood is very absorbent. Paint the inside of the vase liberally, being careful not to paint over the top edge, which should be left bare. Mix the turquoise for the outside with 50% green and 50% blue. Paint it quickly to avoid patchiness, leaving the incised lines bare.

Now that you have completed the vase you are ready to make the flowers and leaves. We show you how to do this in another project, which begins on the next page.

WOODEN FLOWERS

MATERIALS

To make the flowers shown *below* you will need:

Above, saucepan; aluminium foil; rubber gloves.

You will also need the following from the list on page 35: scraps of plywood remaining from the vase; dowel; wooden balls; wood glue; waterproof drawing inks in purple, brown, dark green, yellow and carmine; small vice; coping saw; carbon paper; sandpaper; craft knife; chisel; masking tape; ruler.

To complete the wooden sculpture we began on page 35, in this lesson we show you how make the stylised leaves and flowers that go in the vase.

The vase contains four different types of leaves and one type of flower (each of which is identified in the diagram on page 42). For this project we have made the following: one each of leaves A, C and D; five of leaf B; and four flowers. Before you begin the project you may wish to plan your own combination — for example you could reduce the number of leaf B and make more of leaf A — but do make certain you have enough materials to do this before starting work.

All the leaves and the flowers have stalks that are made in the same way, although the thickness of the dowel that is used varies for the different types. To achieve the best results in your arrangement you should vary the lengths of the stalks so that the leaves and flowers stand at different heights in the vase.

CREATING A SCULPTURE

The word 'sculpture' is defined in the dictionary as a representation in the round of objects or abstract designs, carved in stone or wood or cast in metal. However, this rather reinforces the idea that sculpting requires specialist techniques and materials generally beyond the reach of most of us. This idea is often allied to another misconception — that sculptures are usually made on a grand scale and belong in parks or public buildings. There are, however, numerous examples of sculptures that have been designed on a smaller scale for the home. In addition, many sculptures have been created from components designed for other purposes, and in this lesson we demonstrate one way in which this can be achieved. There are any number of objects around you that can be used to make a sculpture. All you need to do is abandon any preconceived ideas you may have about what materials and objects are meant to be used for.

THE TEMPLATE

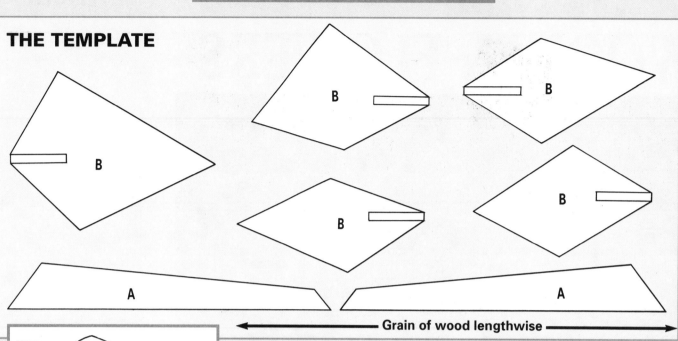

Grain of wood lengthwise

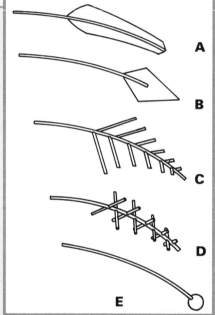

A

B

C

D

E

PREPARING THE DOWEL

You can adapt the method for steaming the dowel for the stalks (described below) as you wish. You can bend the end of the rod rather than the middle, and vary the angle of the curve. However, do not attempt to make the curve too acute or the wood will snap.

1 Cut a piece of dowel to the required length with the coping saw. Fill the saucepan with water to a depth of about 50mm (2in) and rest the dowel across the top. Cover both the dowel and pan with a piece of foil, sealing it as well as possible. Bring the water to a vigorous boil and leave the dowel to steam for at least 15 minutes.

2 Put on a pair of rubber gloves and remove the dowel from the pan. Holding it at either end, gently bend it into a curve. Hold it in this position for a minute or two until it has cooled.

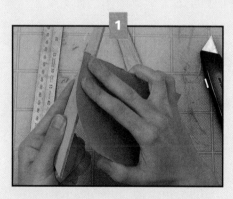

1 To make leaf type A, enlarge the two templates (marked A) to 200% and then enlarge the copy again to 132%. Transfer to a piece of plywood with carbon paper and a pencil. Make sure you place the templates along the grain of the wood. Cut out the pieces and sand the edges.

2 Bend a 400mm (16in) length of $^{1}/_{4}$in dowel so that the curve is at one end and the other end remains straight for 240mm (9$^{7}/_{16}$in). (See Preparing the dowel, *above.*) Place one side of the leaf along the stalk and, if there are gaps, pare the edge with the craft knife until it fits snugly. Repeat with the other side of the leaf and tape the two sides tightly along the stalks, as shown. The sides of the leaf should make an angle of about 105° when viewed from the end (see diagram, *far right*).

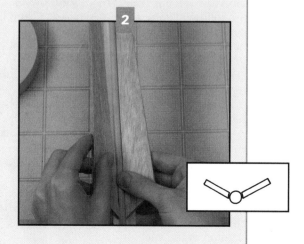

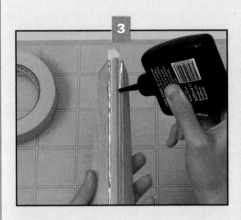

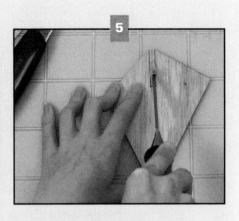

3 Fold both sides of the leaf back, using the tape as a hinge, and run glue down the edge of the plywood next to the stem.

4 Fold the sides back into place and tape them tightly into position with two pieces of tape across the leaf. Put the leaf to one

side until the glue has dried and then remove the masking tape.

5 To make leaf type B (there are five in various shapes and sizes) enlarge the templates and transfer them to the plywood as you did in step 1. Cut out the shapes and sand the edges. To

make the groove, use the craft knife to cut along the lines that form a rectangle at the bottom of the leaf, cutting into the top layer of ply only. If you wish, you can use the ruler as a guide. Use the chisel to remove the top layer of wood. Turn the leaf over and repeat on the other side.

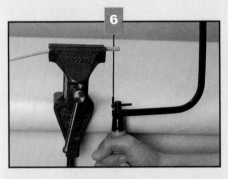

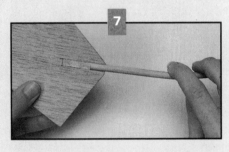

6 Bend a piece of ¼in dowel and clamp it into the vice. With the coping saw, cut a small V-shaped groove in the top of the dowel and then saw a slot 40mm (1½in) in length down the dowel, taking care to keep the slot centred.

7 Sand any rough edges of the dowel and the inside of the slot, as shown. Push the leaf on to the stalk. The stalk will splay out a little, but if it seems about to split, take it apart and sand the inside of the slot a bit more until the stalk pushes 'home'.

8 Disassemble the leaf and stalk and glue the groove on both sides of the leaf. Push the stalk on, wipe any excess glue away with a damp rag and tape the stalk ends firmly down to the leaf on both sides. Leave it to dry.

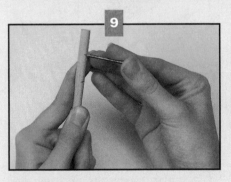

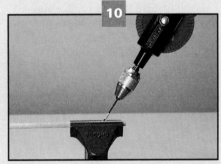

9 To make leaf shape C, bend a 420mm (16¾in) length of ⁵⁄₁₆in dowel for the stalk. Lay it flat and, starting from the top, make pencil marks along the dowel at 2, 4.5, 6.75, 9.5, 12.5, 15.75, 19.25, 23 and 26.75cm (¾, 1¾, 2⅝, 3¾, 5, 6⅜, 7½, 9⅛, 10½in) . Turn the stalk over and mark it on the other side, half way

between each of your previous marks. Make an indentation on each mark to stop the drill bit slipping when you do the next step.

10 Clamp the stalk in the vice and, using the ³⁄₃₂ drill bit, drill holes at an angle of 60° degrees to the stalk, as shown. Do not drill

HELPFUL HINT

When you are drilling the stalk, you can put a 'tape stopper' on the bit to guide you, so that you do not drill too far into the wood. Simply stick a piece of masking tape around the drill bit, with the bottom edge about 10mm (½in) from the end of the bit. To drill the holes in the stalk, you might find it easier to begin the hole at a 90° angle and, once it is started, tilt the drill to the correct angle.

right through to the other side. Re-clamp the stalk as you work down it. Turn it over and drill the holes on the other side, making certain that the angle is 60°. Change the drill bit to ⅛ and re-drill the holes. Sand the stalk smooth.

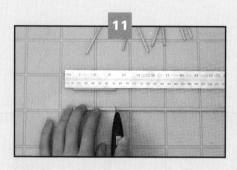

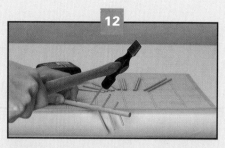

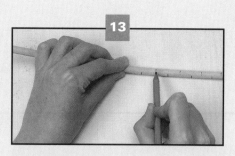

11 Cut a length of $^1/_8$ dowel into nine pairs of pieces, each 12mm (½in) longer than the last (that is, two pieces of 25mm (1in), two of 37mm (1⅜in), two of 49mm (2in), and so on). The best way to cut this thin dowel is to roll it back and forward with the craft knife in place until the dowel snaps easily.

12 Squirt wood glue into the hole at the top of the stalk and put in one of the shortest pieces of dowel. Knock it into place with the hammer. Turn the stalk and put the remaining short piece in the first hole on this side. Work down the stalk, first on one side and then on the other, as shown. Make certain

you graduate the different lengths so that your longest pair is towards the bottom.

13 To make leaf shape D, bend a 330mm (13¼in) length of $^5/_{16}$ dowel. Lay it flat and, starting at the top, make marks at 7, 19, 34, 52, 73, 97, 124 and 154mm (¼, ¾, 1⁵⁄₁₆, 2¹⁄₁₆, 2⅞, 3¾, 4⅞, 6⅛in). Turn the stalk 90° and mark halfway between the previous marks. Make an indentation as you did in step 9.

14 Clamp the stalk in the vice and, starting with the $^3/_{32}$ bit, drill holes at right angles to the stalk and all the way through it. Drill out again with the $^1/_8$ bit. Sand the stalk until it is smooth.

15 Cut a length of 1/8 dowel into 8 pairs of pieces, starting at 25mm (1in) long and increasing in length by 8mm (⅜in) for each pair. Squirt some glue into the holes in the stalk and, starting with the top, hammer in the branches so that there is an equal length on each side. Wipe off the excess glue.

16 To make the flower, bend a length of $^3/_{16}$ dowel and clamp a wooden ball tightly in the vice. Using the $^1/_{16}$ bit first, then the $^1/_8$ and finally the $^1/_4$, drill a hole in the ball to a depth of 5mm (³⁄₁₆in).

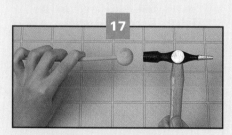

17 Squirt glue into the hole and gently hammer the ball on to the stalk. Wipe off the excess glue.

18 Paint the leaves and flowers carefully with inks as you did for the vase. The purple, brown, red, dark green and pink (carmine) should be used straight from the bottle. For the ochre, add a tiny drop of brown ink to the yellow. The acid green colour is made by adding a drop of dark green ink to the yellow.

To make it easier to arrange the leaves and flowers in the vase, press a large piece of plasticine into the bottom. The plasticine should be deep enough to hold the stalks in an upright position. You will find that you can then make any arrangement you wish without unbalancing the sculpture.

SCULPTURE AND 3-D

WOODEN JIGSAW

Our colourful parrot jigsaw is designed to be both a sturdy educational toy for a young child and an attractive decorative object for the home. Making the puzzle will give you useful experience in basic woodworking techniques.

Making a puzzle is just as much fun as solving one, and it is something that older children can do with adult supervision. The wooden jigsaw you will make in this lesson is called an 'outline' puzzle, in which each piece represents a separate object — such as the beak — or part of an object — such as the tail. This makes it very suitable for young children, although it should not be given to children under the age of three years as some of the pieces are quite small.

Materials and techniques

The best wood to use is 6mm (¼in) birch plywood, as it is extremely easy to cut and sands well. This can be bought at any timber merchants, as can the hardboard for the backing. As you will only need small pieces your supplier may well have some suitable off-cuts. The paint we recommend is Plaka poster colour, but any water-based paint or (for a transparent effect) wood stain, can be used, as long as it is non-toxic. The important thing to remember is that the paint or stain should be well sealed, and you should therefore apply three coats of varnish at the final stage.

Before you begin the project you will need to make a sawing platform (see next page), and this will give you some valuable practice in using the fretsaw. Clamped to your work surface, the sawing platform will protect it from damage and allow free movement when you are sawing around the various shapes. Hold the saw upright, at a right angle to the work, with the metal 'U' shape in line with your forearm.

MATERIALS

To make the jigsaw puzzle shown *below left* you will need:

Above, three sheets of sandpaper, medium grade, fine grade 150 and extra fine grade 240; spraymount repositioning adhesive; 25mm (1in) panel pin; white spirit; hammer; pliers.

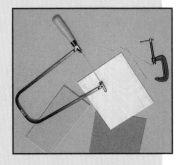

Above, one piece of 6mm (¼in)-thick birch plywood, 200 x 180mm (8 x 7in); one piece of 6-mm (¼in)-thick hardboard 200 x 180mm (8 x 7in); small G-clamp; piece of MDF (medium density fibreboard), approximately 230 x 130mm (9 x 5in); fretsaw; Hobbies size 6 fretsaw blade plus 3 extra fine to medium blades.

Above, Plaka poster paints in red, orange, yellow, green, blue and brown; paintbrush, size 8; scalpel; decorator's brush, 25mm (1in); jam jar; plate, for mixing; satin-finish polyurethane or acrylic varnish; wood glue.

THE TEMPLATES

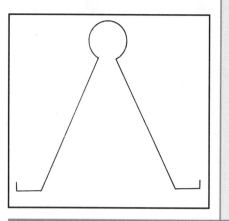

MAKING A SAWING PLATFORM

A sawing platform is very similar to a jeweller's peg and is used in much the same way. It provides a platform for resting your work on, for example when using the fretsaw. To make the platform, photocopy the template (*above*) at 200 % and attach it to the piece of MDF with spraymount. Attach the G-clamp to the edge of your work surface and cut out the 'key' shape. Remove the template with white spirit.

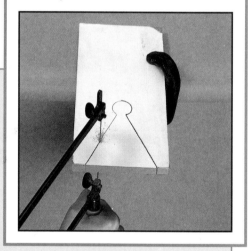

hour. Dampening the wood raises the grain, and allows you to produce a really smooth surface. Sand the wood again when it is dry using the extra-fine sandpaper.

1 Choose the better side of the plywood and use the fine grade sandpaper to smooth the surface. Always stroke the sandpaper along the direction of the wood grain. Wipe over the wood with a damp cloth and leave to dry for half an

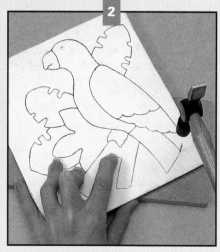

2 Photocopy the template for the jigsaw at 150% and stick it on to the plywood with spraymount. If necessary, trim the edges of the paper. Put the plywood on the sawing platform and hammer a panel pin through the plywood at the tip of the parrot's tail so that only the top 5mm (3/16in) of the pin is above the surface. This gives you the starting point for sawing.

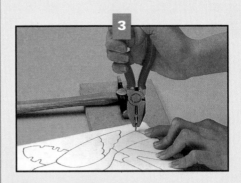

3 Remove the panel pin with a pair of pliers, holding them at a 90° angle. Take care not to damage the plywood.

HELPFUL HINT

To ensure that the fretsaw blade is fitted as taut as possible, you may find it necessary to shorten the blade. To do this, simply cut off 3mm (1/8in) from one of the ends.

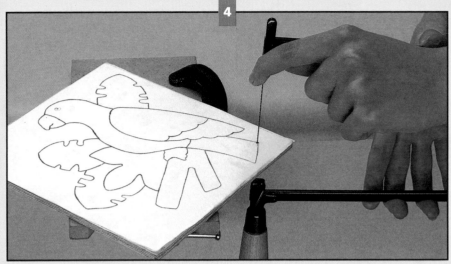

4 Fix your sawing platform to the edge of the table with the G-clamp. Attach the fretsaw blade to one end of the fretsaw and thread it through the starting hole in the wood. Make sure the teeth of the blade are pointing downwards. Now fix the other end of the blade to the saw, making sure it is taut. Screw the blade in place, using the pliers to tighten the wing nut if necessary.

5 Cut along the lines of the template, using gentle pressure and holding the saw vertically. Cut straight up the whole of the outside edge of the wing first, then come down the other side and across the 'scalloped' edge of the wing feathers. Follow the bends by turning the work piece rather than the saw.

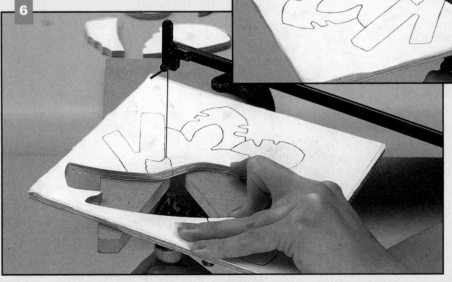

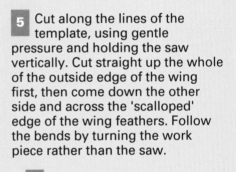

6 When you come to a sharp corner, keep on sawing up and down as you turn the work piece, but do not push the blade forward. This should take you easily around the corners. Continue sawing until you have cut out all the pieces, then peel off the template. Wipe the surface of each piece with white spirit to remove any remaining glue. Lightly sand the back of all the pieces.

7 Varnish the frame and leave to dry for about six hours.

8 When the varnish is dry, apply wood glue to the back of the the puzzle frame, smoothing it over the whole surface with your finger. Turn the frame the right way up and stick it on to the hessian-backed side of the hardboard. Leave to dry under a few heavy books for approximately six hours.

9 While the glue is drying, lay out the puzzle pieces and paint them with poster paints. To make the orange colour, mix up some yellow with a touch of red. When the head is dry, mark in the parrot's eye with the blue paint. Leave to dry, then apply a coat of varnish to each piece. When the glue on the puzzle frame is completely dry, apply another coat of varnish to the frame and the puzzle pieces. It is not necessary to varnish the hardboard, the sides of the pieces or frame, or underneath the puzzle pieces.

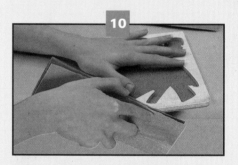

10 Wait for the varnish to dry, then apply a third coat to give added durability and finish. Leave to dry. Using medium grade sandpaper, then fine grade, smooth down the four edges of the puzzle. The edges are quite rough so you will need to do quite a bit of sanding to get them smooth. Finally, round off the sharp corners to give the puzzle a finishing touch.

Once you have made the parrot jigsaw you may wish to create some designs of your own. The main point to consider is that you need to keep the shapes of the individual puzzle pieces as simple as possible, without too many sharp corners or very narrow pieces.

SCULPTURE AND 3-D

WEATHER VANE

MATERIALS

To make the weather vane shown *below left* you will need:

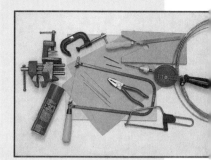

Above, one piece 6mm (1/4in) exterior quality birch plywood, 300 x 330mm (12 x 13in); vice; G-clamp; file; hand drill and 3/32in and 1/8in bits; fretsaw with Hobbies size 6 blade; junior hacksaw; pliers; fencing wire, 3.1mm (1/8in) in diameter; spraymount repositioning adhesive; sandpaper, medium and fine grade; sawing platform.

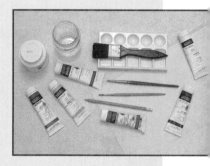

Above, graphite paper; pencil; palette; acrylic paints in red oxide, raw umber, Turner's yellow, ceruleun blue, chromium oxide green; acrylic gesso; 40mm (1 1/2in) decorator's brush; paintbrushes, medium and fine; water jar.

Above, piece of wood 200 x 200mm x 50mm (8 x 8 x 2in); wood glue; hammer; linseed oil; one 50mm (2in) masonry nail; panel pins.

The design for our cheerful weather vane is based on the traditional rooster motif that has for centuries been a popular figure in folk art. Made of wood, painted with acrylics and varnished, the weather vane would make an attractive garden or patio ornament.

Before the time of weather forecasts, the weather vane was an essential tool for farmers. The weather vane pointed in the direction of the prevailing wind and was an aid in deciding when to plant and harvest.

The rooster design originated over 1000 years ago on church steeples as a reminder to people not to deny their faith, as St Peter did when the cock crowed three times. In the Middle Ages these stationary symbols were made into weather vanes, and later, in America, farmers adopted the idea for use on the tops of houses, barns and shops, in the form of various animals or even human figures. We have used the traditional

'weathercock' design and painted it in muted colours for a 'folk art' style of decorative painting.

The exterior-quality birch ply, the sealing coat of gesso and the acrylic paints all contribute to making the weather vane weather proof, and to prolong its life even further you could give it a coat of acrylic varnish. Linseed oil will preserve the wooden base and will allow the wood to mellow with age.

Any piece of off-cut wood can be used to make the base as long as you cut the top square. The heavier the wood the better, so a piece of hardwood, such as oak, would be ideal.

THE TEMPLATE

1 Photocopy the template at 200%, then enlarge again at 140%. Make another copy. Stick one on to the plywood with spraymount. Fix the sawing platform to the edge of the work surface with a G-clamp. Fit a blade on the fretsaw and cut the plywood along the dotted line. Place the piece of plywood with the rooster design on the sawing platform and cut around the outline. Work carefully around sharp corners, turning, but not pushing the wood.

2 Cut the piece of plywood with the design of the letters in two pieces to make working easier. Cut out the letters, starting and finishing at the same point.

3 Clamp the foot of the rooster in a vice. Fit the 3/32in bit in the hand drill and drill through the middle ply, holding the drill absolutely vertical — it is essential

to the working of the weather vane that the hole is centrally positioned and straight.

Drill slowly to a depth of 2cm (3/4in), using the dashes on the template as a guide. Check the depth of the cut by marking the drill bit with your thumbnail before you remove it from the wood, and matching the length against the dashes on the template. Using the

same bit, drill holes in the letters in the positions marked on the template to a depth of 5mm (3/16in), again marking the drill bit with your nail to check the depth.

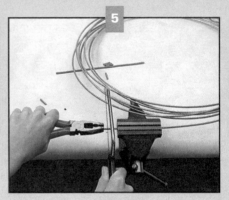

4 Remove the template from the rooster. Sand both surfaces and the edges, first with medium grade and then with fine grade sandpaper. Wipe off the dust. Paint with one coat of acrylic gesso. Do the same for the letters. Wash the brush well with water.

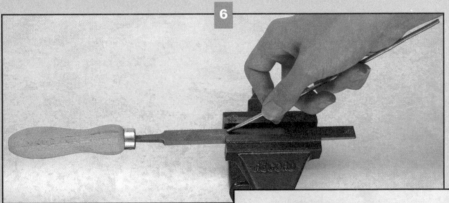

5 Clamp the wire in the vice and hold the free end with a pair of pliers. With the hacksaw, cut off one piece 200mm (7⅞in) long, and six pieces 15mm (⅝in) long.

6 Clamp the file in the vice and remove the burrs on both ends of all the short pieces of wire. File one end of the long piece in the same way, and continue filing the other end until it is fully rounded (this will allow the wire to pivot in the wooden base).

7 Insert the end of the long wire with the flat end into the hole in the leg of the rooster and tap the wire in very gently with a hammer.

Using the second photocopy and a sheet of graphite paper, transfer the markings on to the rooster with a pencil. Start painting on one side starting from the top. Use the brushes fairly dry; the small brush to outline the areas of colour, and the medium brush to fill in the areas. Use the red, yellow, green, blue and brown (raw umber) straight from the tube, and mix the orange for the beak and some of the feathers from yellow and red. Add a few strokes of orange to the yellow areas, and leave a small white circle for the eye. Outline the eye with orange, and put a tiny dot of brown in the middle. Give the wire two coats of brown paint. The paint dries quickly, so you can paint the other side almost immediately.

Paint the letters with one coat of brown paint.

8 Mark the centre of the base by drawing diagonal lines across the corners with a pencil (use the straight edge of the off-cut plywood if you don't have a ruler). Drill a hole in the centre with the 1/8in bit to a depth of 4cm (1⁵/8in).

Tap the short pieces of wire into the holes in the letters and mark their positions on the lines close to the corners, as shown, with pencil. Drill holes for the letters with the 3/32in bit to a depth of 1cm (3/8in). Sand the wood with medium and then fine grade sandpaper to erase the pencil lines and smooth the edges and drill-holes. Put a little wood glue on the ends of the wires and the base of the letters and insert them in the holes.

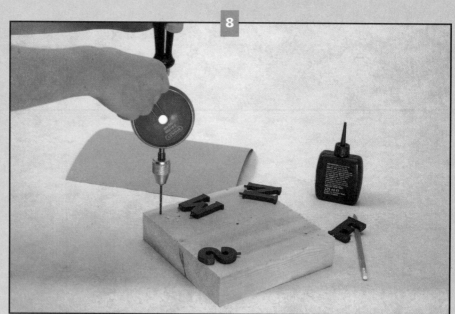

If you intend to make full use of your weather vane, do make certain that you place it in an open position in the garden so that it gives a correct indication of the wind direction – preferably somewhere where you can see it from inside the house.

9 Give all surfaces of the base a coat of linseed oil and allow to dry for 2 days. Give another coat of linseed oil and again allow to dry.

Clamp a panel pin in the vice and cut a 5mm (3/16in) length off the top. Drop the top piece into the central hole of the base, with the head of the pin uppermost. Push the masonry nail into the hole and hammer it in gently to lodge the panel pin into the wood, taking care not to drive it in too far. Insert the wire of the rooster into the hole.

SCULPTURE AND 3-D

KITCHEN BLACKBOARD

Our kitchen blackboard with its colourful surround of acrobatic cats will give you plenty of opportunity to refine your skills with a fretsaw. The cats are stained with water-soluble wood stains that yield rich, mellow colours.

We have already used a fretsaw in both our jigsaw and weather vane projects. However, to cut out the cat frame for this project you need quite a lot of skill with the fretsaw and quite a lot of patience! After you have cut out the centre piece from the frame, we show you how to reverse the fretsaw blade to cope with the complicated bits. It has been known for a fretsaw blade to snap when you are cutting out awkward shapes, and for this reason we suggest that you have at least five blades to hand.

We have used water-soluble wood stains (available from art shops and some hardware shops) to colour the cats. These are mixed from small quantities of powdered pigments. A little goes a long way — if you find you have mixed too much you can store the remainder in screw top jars. Test out the colours on a piece of scrap wood before using them, and practise doing the markings. The masking fluid stops the stain from creeping along the grain of the wood from one cat to another, but nevertheless it is a good idea to paint carefully around these areas with a fairly dry brush to ensure a clean finish.

MATERIALS

To make the blackboard shown *below left* you will need:

Above, piece of hardboard 39 x 48cm (15$\frac{1}{2}$ x 19in); piece of 4mm ($\frac{5}{32}$in) birch plywood 50.5 x 56cm (20 x 22in); piece of 12mm ($\frac{1}{2}$in) plywood 21 x 31cm (8 x 12in); carbon paper; sandpaper, fine, medium and coarse; 30cm (11$\frac{1}{2}$in) fretsaw and 5 medium woodcutting blades; masking tape; pencil; vice; rasp; pliers; bradawl; small hammer; epoxy resin glue.

Above, blackboard paint; masking fluid; watersoluble pigment stains, brown, black, orange, yellow; plaka paint, brown; 4 jam jars; brushes, 1 medium flat, 2 fine watercolour, two 25mm (1in) decorator's brushes; satin varnish; wood glue; 2 hanging hooks; 4 small nails; white spirit; methylated spirits.

TEMPLATE AND CUTTING GUIDE

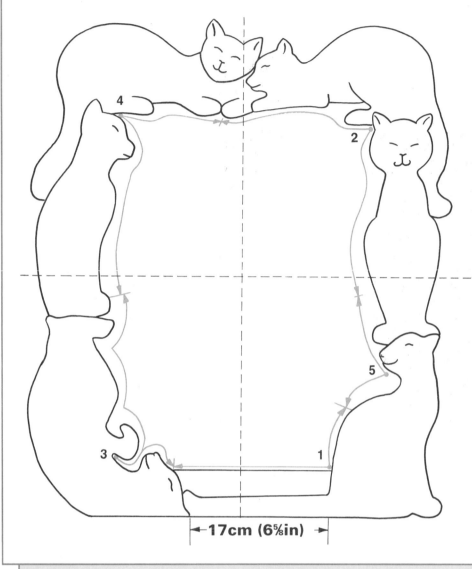

←17cm (6⅝in)→

1 Cover the edges of the hardboard with masking tape and, using a decorator's brush, paint blackboard paint over the board, brushing it on in one direction and smoothing it out in the opposite direction. Leave to dry. Apply three more coats, aiming for a smooth finish.

2 Smooth one side of the plywood with medium grade sandpaper. Photocopy each quarter of the template at 200% and then at 200% again. Stick the photocopies together. Trim along the base of the design and line it up along one of the shorter sides of the wood (on the sanded side). Tape it in position. Trace the design on to the wood using carbon paper.

3 Place the wood on a work surface and fit a blade into the fretsaw. Starting at the top righthand corner, cut as far as the fretsaw will allow around the outline, missing out the tight corner near the base of the tail. Keep the blade upright and cut on the down stroke only. Remove the fretsaw and cut from the base to meet the first cut.

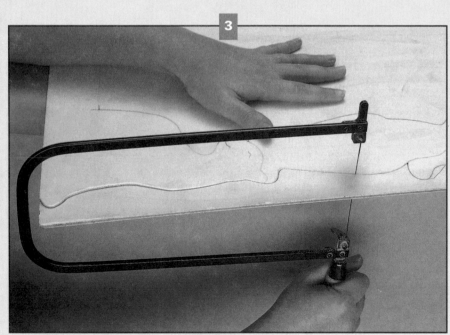

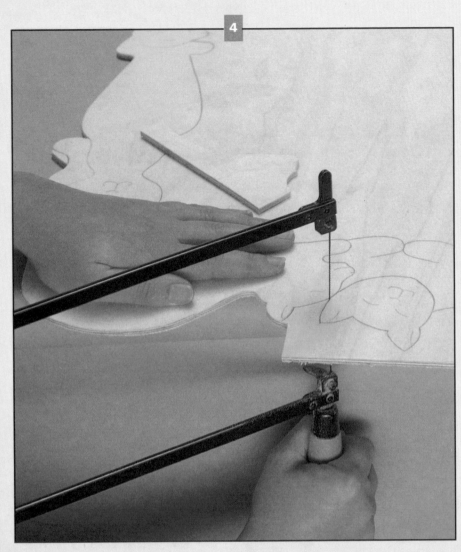

4 Continue cutting around the outside outline, missing out tight corners, or cutting separate pieces. When you have gone around the whole outline, cut into the small remaining areas.

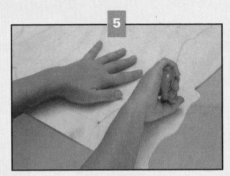

5 With the bradawl, make holes in the positions marked on the cutting guide.

6 Unscrew one end of the blade, thread it through hole 1 and re-fit in the fretsaw. Cut around the inside outline following the cutting guide. Stop where indicated, and thread the blade through hole 2. Continue until you have cut out the central piece. Then cut out the remaining small areas. For some of these you will need to use the fretsaw with the blade reversed (see Helpful Hint, *below left*).

HELPFUL HINT

When you are cutting with a fretsaw, keep the blade vertical and use a straight up and down motion, cutting the wood only on the downstroke. If it is too difficult to cut exactly on the line, cut on the outside of the line. The surplus wood can be trimmed away with a file and sandpaper. Start cutting from the edge of the wood — for the long outlines you will need to make cuts from each end to meet in the middle.

To cut the awkward corners in step 6, remove the blade from the fretsaw and reverse it. When cutting with a reversed blade, the saw moves towards you, rather than away from you.

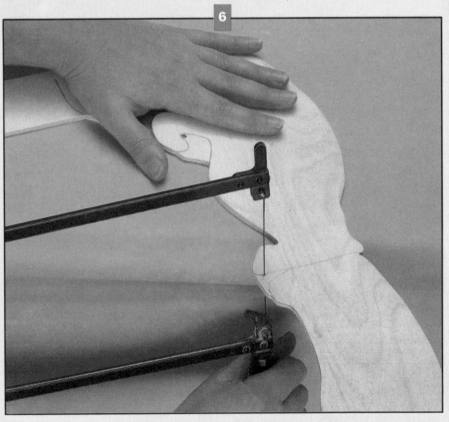

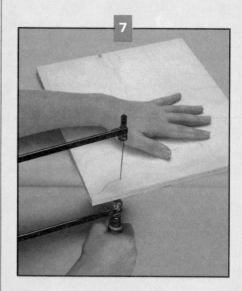

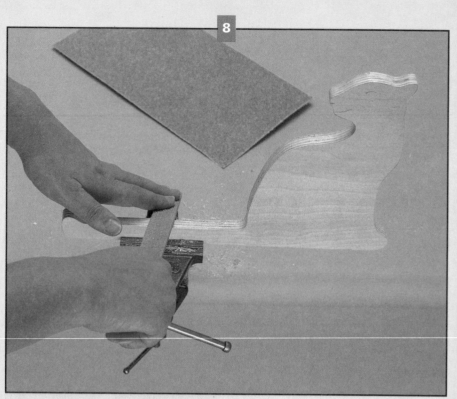

7 Use the template and the carbon paper to transfer the outline of the cat with a long tail at the bottom righthand corner on to a piece of 12mm (1/2in) ply. Cut round the outline with a fretsaw.

8 Secure the vice to the work surface, and clamp the tail of the cat in the vice. Using a rasp, shave the tail at an angle so that the back is lower than the front (this will form a ledge for the chalk). Sand all the edges.

HELPFUL HINT

To protect the face of the wood, insert a scrap piece of plywood in the vice when you are using the rasp.

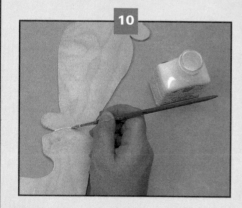

9 Secure the frame in the vice and sand all the edges carefully.

10 Using a fine brush, paint the lines between the cats with a line of masking fluid. Wash the brush.

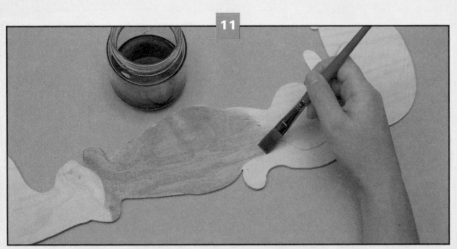

11 Mix half a teaspoon of each pigment in a separate jam jar half full of warm water. With the large brush, paint the yellow cats with the yellow stain, keeping the brush quite dry near the masking fluid lines so that the stain does not seep into the adjacent area.

12 Paint the orange cats on the frame, again being careful at the edges. Paint the long-tailed cat orange. Leave to dry for 5 minutes.

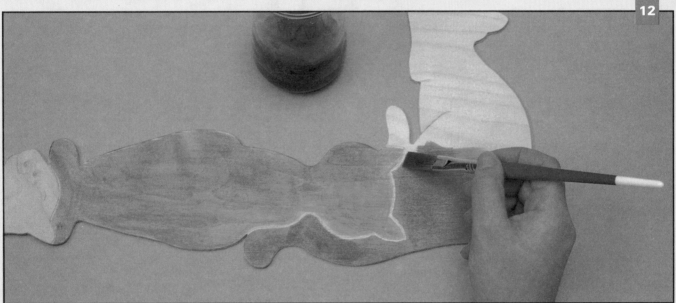

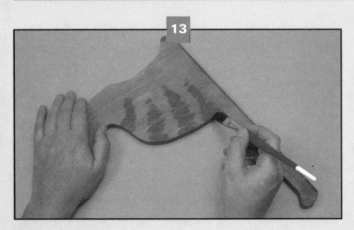

13 With a fairly dry brush, paint the markings on the long-tailed cat with a mix of orange and black. Paint the markings on the upside down yellow cat with a mix of yellow and brown. Paint the frame just above the long tail with blackboard paint. Leave to dry.

14 Remove the masking fluid with your finger, or with an eraser. Using a fine line, paint these lines with brown Plaka paint. Also paint the ears, facial details and paws of the cats. Varnish the frame and the long-tailed cat with two coats of varnish, allowing each coat to dry overnight.

15 Remove the masking tape from the hardboard and sand the edges of the board. Put the cat frame face down and lay the blackboard face down on top. Mark the outline of the board on the frame. Remove the board and spread wood glue on the frame on the overlap area. Glue the board to the frame, and put a heavy weight on top. Leave to dry overnight.

16 Use epoxy resin to glue the hooks to the top of the board (see manufacturer's instructions).

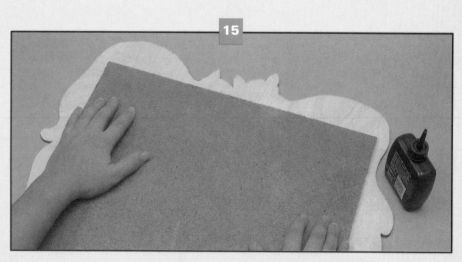

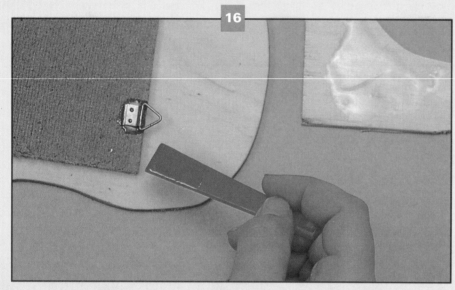

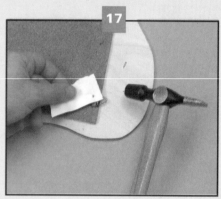

17 Hammer the tiny nails in place to hold the hooks more securely (pierce the nail into a piece of paper so that you can hold it in position more easily).

18 Stick the long-tailed cat to the front of the frame with wood glue, weight it down and leave to dry overnight.

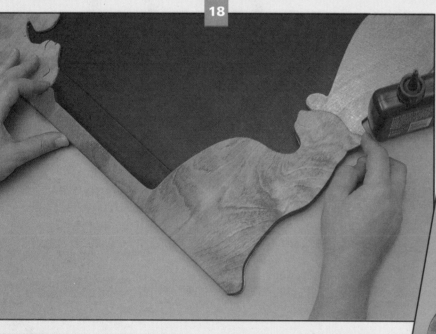

Your blackboard will make an eye-catching feature for your kitchen. You can use it for shopping lists, or to write reminders to yourself, or for family messages.

SCULPTURE AND 3-D

FLYING DRAGON

MATERIALS

To make the dragon shown *below left* **you will need:**

Above, 9mm (³/₈in) plywood, 570 x 170mm (23 x 7in); 2 pieces 4mm (⁵/₃₂in) plywood, 450 x 285mm(18 x 11in); 350mm (14in) length of 10mm (³/₈in) diameter dowel; small screw hook; 3m (3yds) kite string; acrylic gesso primer; acrylic paints, white, emerald green, light emerald green, yellow light hansa, red, black.

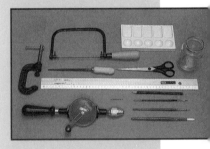

Above, coping saw; 5cm (2in) G-clamp; round (or half round) file; 500mm (20in) ruler; pencil; palette; jam jar; hand drill and 1.5mm (¹/₁₆in) drill bit; scissors; brushes, sizes 1, 4 and 10.

The construction of our endearing flying dragon depends on achieving a perfect balance between the wings — so that a slight current of air causes the wings to flap and the body to move up and down as if the dragon was flying.

The dragon is a legendary beast, usually represented as a huge, winged fire-breathing reptile. In Christian art the dragon is usually associated with evil, but in the Far East it has benign associations. In the Chinese horoscope, for example, the Dragon year is considered to be the most lucky of the twelve. The dragon in our project is without doubt one of the kindlier beasts.

Perfect balance
The cutting and painting of the pieces is straightforward. When drilling the holes it is important that the distance between the holes on the body is the same as the distance between the holes that are drilled on the edge of the wings, so that when the string is threaded through to join the

pieces, it does not cause any tension. If you design your own flying creature, make sure that the holes on the body are above the centre of the piece.

The position of the second set of holes on the wings is indicated on the template, but the exact position can only be determined when you make the dragon. Before you drill the holes, take time to adjust the position of the strings in order to get the balance right — the method is explained in step 15 on page 64.

Creatures great or small
You could amend our template and create your own design for a dragon. Alternatively, you could make another flying creature — perhaps a bat, bird, butterfly or moth, or a menacing wasp.

THE TEMPLATES

BODY

Enlarge the body at 200%, then again at 149%

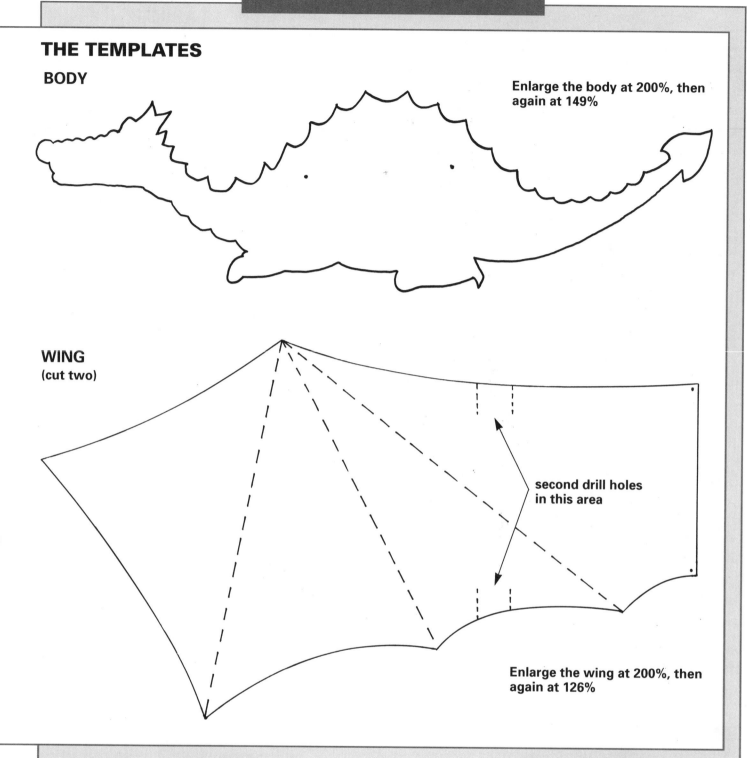

WING
(cut two)

second drill holes in this area

Enlarge the wing at 200%, then again at 126%

1 Enlarge the templates on a photocopier at the percentages given. Cut around the outlines. Place the body template on the 9mm (³⁄₈in) plywood and draw around it with pencil. Go over the outline again if necessary.

2 Secure the wood to the table with a G-clamp and cut around the outline with the coping saw, moving the position of the wood and the direction of the blade (see salad servers) as necessary.

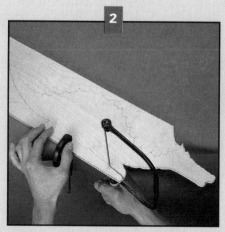

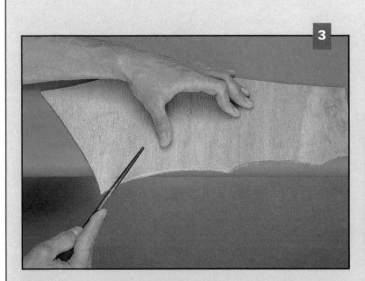

3 Draw the outline of the wing template on both pieces of 4mm (5/32in) plywood, then cut out the wings with the coping saw. Smooth the edges of the wings and the body with the round file.

4 Paint the body and wing pieces with acrylic gesso straight from the pot using the size 10 brush. When dry, apply two coats of emerald green acrylic paint.

5 Draw the legs and other features in pencil on the body as shown.

6 Paint over the lines and areas as shown with a mix of black and emerald green to give an impression of shadow. Paint the top half of the body a slightly lighter green (using a mix of light emerald green and emerald green).

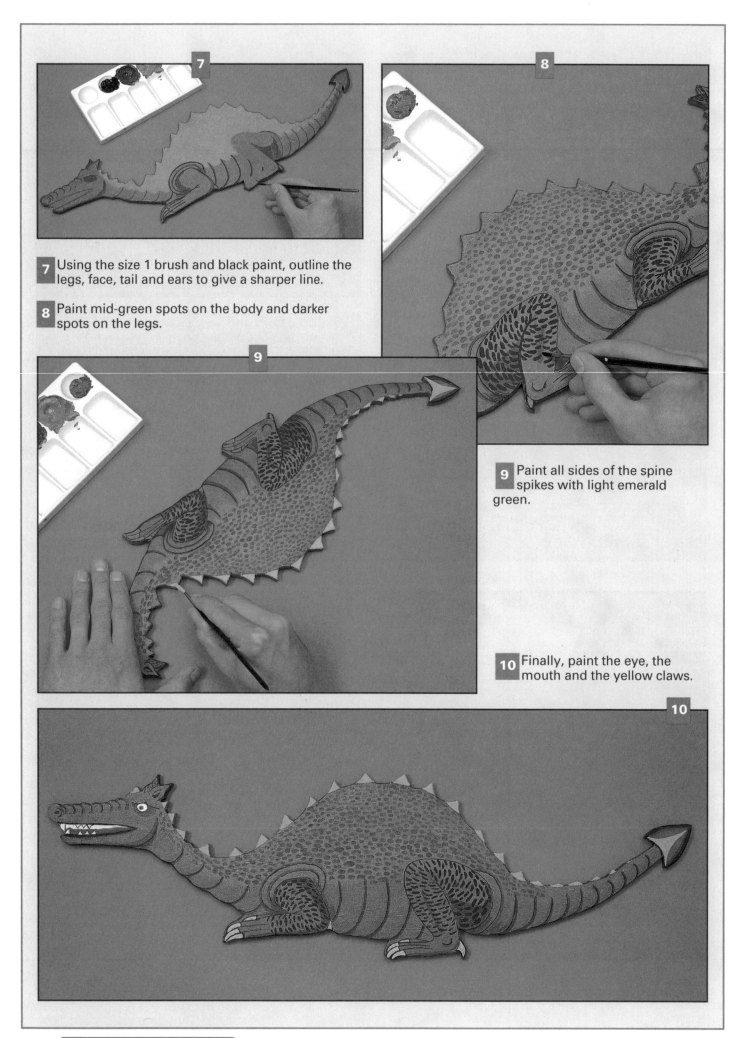

7 Using the size 1 brush and black paint, outline the legs, face, tail and ears to give a sharper line.

8 Paint mid-green spots on the body and darker spots on the legs.

9 Paint all sides of the spine spikes with light emerald green.

10 Finally, paint the eye, the mouth and the yellow claws.

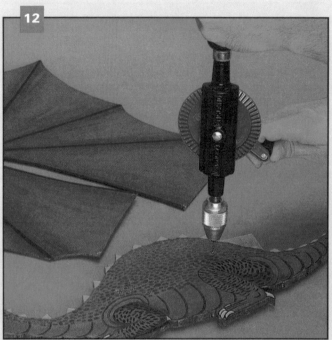

11 Draw pencil lines on both sides of the wings (shown as broken lines on the template), and shade the areas either side of the lines with emerald green darkened with black. Paint over the pencil lines and the front edge of the wing with black paint.

12 Using a scrap of wood to protect the work surface, make a hole at the corner of the wings with the hand drill and the 1.5mm ($^1/_{16}$in) bit in the positions marked on the template. Drill two holes in the body of the dragon, as marked on the template.

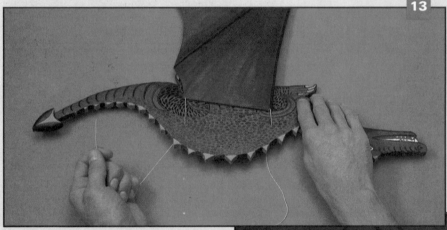

13 Arrange the body and the left wing as shown. Cut a 50cm (20in) length of kite string and thread it through the front hole on the body from beneath, through the front hole on the wing from the top, back up through the rear hole on the wing, then back through the body, as shown.

HELPFUL HINT

The distance between the two holes in the wing and the two holes in the body should be exactly the same.

14 Turn the dragon over and thread the other wing on to the body in the same way. Pull the string taut, but not too tight (the wings should move freely). Tie the ends of the string together with a double knot under the wing, then trim the ends. Cut two 1-metre (1yd) lengths of string and knot the ends of each one together to make a loop.

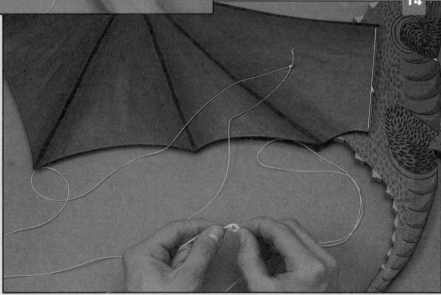

15 Fix the screw hook in the centre of the dowel. Loop one piece of kite string around one end of the rod and one wing about 13-15cm (5-6in) away from the body as shown. Loop the other string on the other side. Adjust the kite strings until you find the point of balance where both wings are horizontal, then mark the positions on the wings, rod and strings.

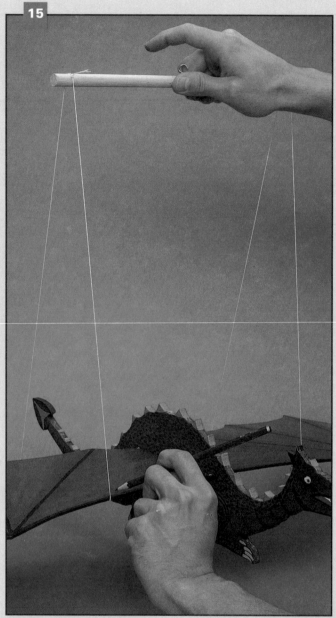

16 Drill a hole either end of the rod in the positions marked, from front to back. Saw off the ends to within 5mm (³/16in) of the holes. Drill a hole on either side of each wing where marked, about 3mm (¹/8in) from the edge. Cut open the loops of string and thread through from the underside of the front of the wing, through the rod, and down into the hole on the other side of the wing. Knot the ends at the points marked, and trim. Repeat on the other wing.

Hang the dragon up in a slight draught. The current of air will gently move the wings and they will flap lugubriously up and down in a dragon-like manner.

SCULPTURE AND 3-D

BLUE FOOTED BOOBY

Our blue footed bird is a stylised version of a fascinating species that inhabits the Galapagos Islands. Sculpted from softwood and brightly finished with enamel paints, it would make an amusing decorative object for the home or office.

All creative ideas have their origins in reality, however that reality may have been altered or distorted. Imagination can only work with material gleaned from observation of the world around us, and the real world is often far more extraordinary than anything we can invent. The Blue Footed Booby (*Sula nebouxii*) is a bird that lives in the Galapagos Islands off South America. As well as its big blue feet, which get bluer the older the bird grows, it has a touching courtship behaviour, in which a male booby presents to the female a selection of nesting

materials — such as guano, seaweed and fishbones — and she chooses her mate according to the quality of the offering. The courtship behaviour of the male is quite spectacular and includes goose-stepping with the tail feathers raised. The idea for our sculpture is based on this unusual bird.

The body has to be shaped into the appropriate form, which is done by making a series of straight cuts into a piece of standard timber. The technique is simple and provided you can visualise three-dimensional shapes, it can be applied to all types of structure.

MATERIALS

To make the bird shown *below left* you will need:

Above, one piece of 2 x 3in softwood, 125mm (5in) long; ³/₄in dowel, 100mm (4in) long; ⁵/₁₆in dowel, 250mm (10in) long; two ³/₈in round brass screws; two M4 ⁵/₃₂in steel washers; two pencils; steel ruler.

Above, vice, with jaws wide enough to take a 45mm (1³/₄in) wide object; wood saw; drill and wood bits ¹/₈ and ⁵/₁₆in; surform plane; craft knife; sandpaper, fine, medium and coarse; wood glue.

Above, round nylon brush, size 6 or 7; bradawl; small screwdriver; sanding sealer; enamel paint in the following colours, gloss black 21, white 22, yellow 69, blue 14; enamel thinner, for cleaning brushes.

1 The block of softwood is used to make the bird's body. Using diagrams **1-5** as a guide, mark off the dotted lines on your wood block, cutting each stage when marked, as described in step 2. (Diagram **6** shows the completed shape.)

Diagrams 1- 6

(all dimensions are in millimetres: 25mm = 1in)

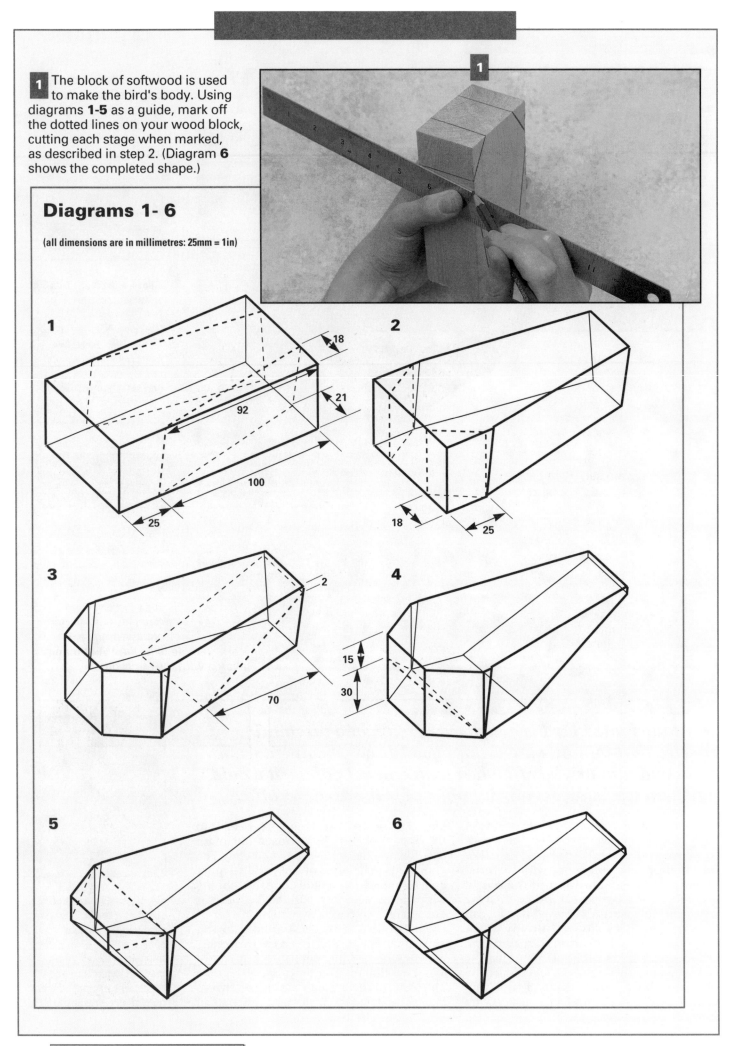

2 Clamp the wood in the vice and saw along the lines you have marked. Try to keep the cuts as straight as possible, and keep the pieces you have cut off the sides — you will need them later for the feet.

3 With the surform plane (see Using the surform plane, *below*), smooth down the rough saw cuts and round off all the corners. If you find it easier, you can use the plane with one hand and hold the block of wood in the other, instead of using the vice. If you do use the vice, you may need to wedge pieces of wood in it to keep the block firm. When you have finished, sand the body until it is smooth and even, starting with coarse grain sandpaper and ending with fine.

USING THE SURFORM PLANE

Holding the handle in your left hand and grasping the top of the plane in your right (or vice versa if you are lefthanded), slide the plane across the surface of the wood. Use forward strokes only; do not attempt to slide it back and forth. The surform works across, as well as with, the grain of the wood. However, it is most effective when used at an angle to the direction you are pushing. Used with the grain, it will plane more gently.

4 Using the craft knife, 'sharpen' the end of the thick dowel to a point as shown, making it slightly off centre. Sand the point smooth.

5 Clamp the dowel in the vice and drill a $5/16$in hole in the flat end, to a depth of 10mm ($3/8$in). Start the hole with the $1/8$in bit and finish it with the $5/16$in bit.

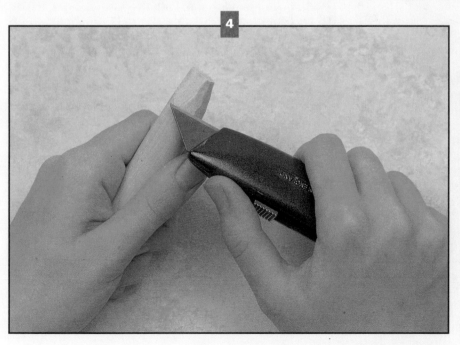

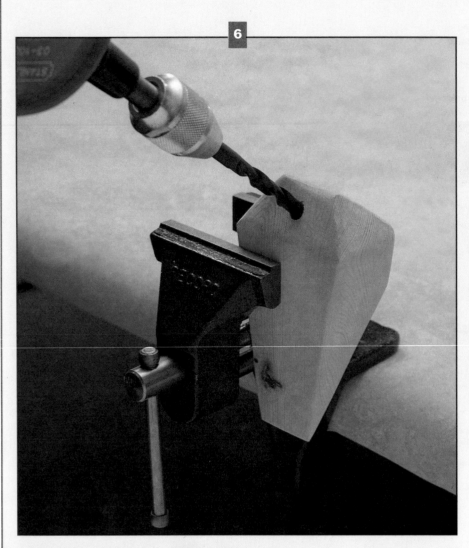

6 Put the body in the vice, as shown, and drill another hole in the same way into the front top side of it, at right angles to the cut surface.

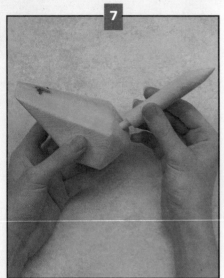

7 Cut a 20mm (3/4in) piece of 5/16in dowel and push it into the neck of the bird and then into the body. If there is a gap between the neck and the body, disassemble the pieces and sand the peg and the flat end of the neck until it fits together.

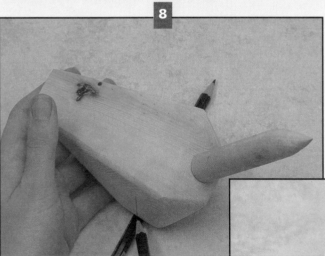

8 Place the body on a pencil, as shown, to find the approximate angle at which it balances. Mark a vertical line on the body at the centre of the pencil and at a right angle to your work surface.

9 Remove the neck and, with the 5/16in drill bit, make two holes approximately 32mm (1 1/4in) apart and 10mm (3/8in) deep in the bottom of the bird, in line with the mark you have made.

TEMPLATE FOR FEET

Photocopy the template below at 125% for one foot.
Then trace your photocopy and reverse it for the other foot.

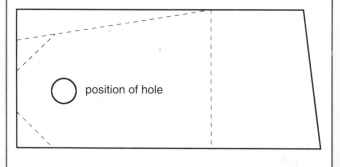

○ position of hole

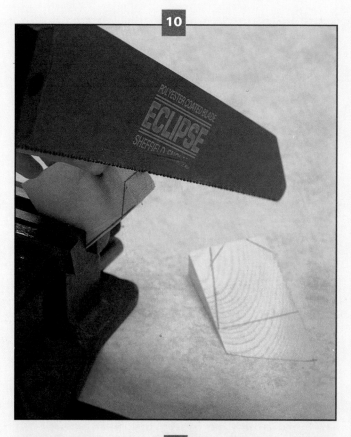

10 To make the feet, photocopy the template and trace it as described *above*. Then transfer the design to the off-cuts you saved in step 2. Cut out one foot from each piece, as shown. Try to match the slope of the wedges so that both feet are the same.

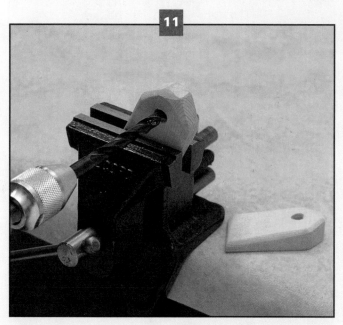

11 Using the ⁵/₁₆in drill bit, drill a hole vertically right through each foot at the point marked on the template. Sand the feet smooth, paying particular attention to the edges.

12 Cut the ⁵/₁₆in dowel into two pieces each 100mm (4in) long. Push them into the holes in the body and then into the holes in the feet. If the bird doesn't stand straight, trim the end of the dowel until it does. Glue all the joints, leave to dry and sand down any excess glue. Paint the whole bird with sanding sealer, taking care to avoid drips. When the sealer has dried rub it down with fine sandpaper.

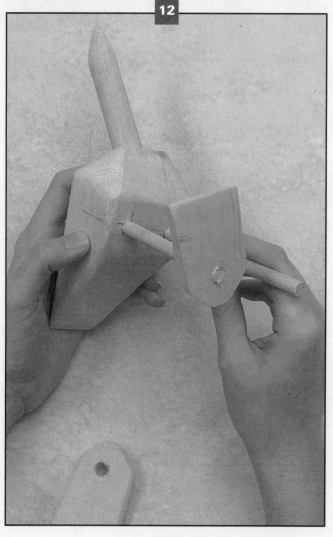

13 With a pencil, draw the lines that separate the white areas from the black areas and the blue legs, and the line round the beak. Paint the black areas first, making a neat line at the edge. Leave to dry and then paint the white areas, painting right up to the black edge. Paint legs, feet and beak; it is not necessary to paint the bottom of the feet. Leave the paint to dry overnight, and longer if possible. When the paint has hardened, rub it down with fine sandpaper and re-paint the whole bird.

14 To complete the bird, make a hole for the position of the eyes with the bradawl and screw the washers into position, making certain they are centred before tightening the screws.

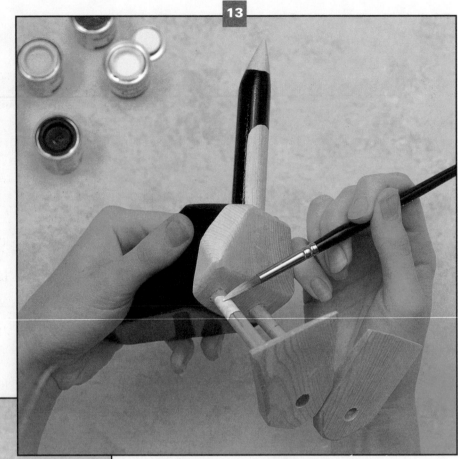

If you wish, you could apply a wood varnish to the bird's body instead of painting it. But if you do, you should still paint the feet blue in keeping with the name Blue Footed Booby.

SCULPTURE AND 3-D

THUMB PIANO

In this project we show you how to use your woodworking and metalworking skills to make an African thumb piano that is surprisingly easy to play. Even if you are not musical, it will make an intriguing ornament.

The thumb piano is an African instrument that was developed in the last century. It belongs to the largest category of musical instruments in Africa, the idiophones. These are self-sounding instruments which have a series of thin, flexible keys, usually made from bamboo, wood or hammered iron. The keys are always arranged on a flat soundboard, but they can vary in number and the way they are arranged. The soundboard is invariably made of wood, and can be fan-shaped, box-shaped or bell-shaped.

The number of keys and the way they are arranged on the soundboard varies from region to region. In the Shona region, for example, the treble keys are arranged on the righthand side, and the base keys on the lefthand side. Keys arranged in a staggered manner make melodic patterns easier to play. A thumb piano is played with the thumbs and sometimes one or both forefingers. The thumbs pluck downward and the forefinger upward.

Ringing tones

In Angola and Mozambique wax is attached to the keys to make the instrument ring. A continuous buzzing effect from vibrators attached to the soundboard systematically prolongs the sound.

We have used a guitar back, which is made from ziricote wood, to make the soundbox for our piano. You can use other hardwoods, but don't use one that is too brittle or too thin, or you risk getting cracks in the soundboard. When you plane the edges of the soundboard you will need a shooting board to achieve a perfect 90° angle. You can make this from two pieces of plywood, with a ridge at one end to stop the object sliding off.

MATERIALS

To make the thumb piano shown *below left* you will need:

Above, a guitar back, or ziricote hardwood 3.5mm (¹/₈in) thick, 40 x 25cm (15¾ x 10in); wooden rod 5 x 5 x 650mm (³/₁₆ x ³/₁₆ x 26in); piece of 25mm (1in) broom handle; fretsaw; plane; 10m (11yds) cotton tape; rasp; 25 clothes pegs; 25 rubber bands; wood glue; metal ruler; pencil.

Above, metal saw; four G-clamps; centre punch; compass; shooting board; sawing platform; hand drill; screwdriver; wax; 2mm (¹/₁₆in) and 3mm (¹/₈in) drill bits; small anvil; hammer; metal file; sandpaper; scraper; seven mild steel 35cm (14in) metal rods 5mm (³/₁₆in) diameter; vice; two screws 2.5 x 30mm (¹/₈ x 1³/₁₆in); wire wool.

HELPFUL HINT

Making musical instruments is a specialist form of woodworking, and one that requires infintessimal patience and a drive for perfection. The entire musical sound of an instrument can be critically altered if measurements are even minutely inaccurate.

DIAGRAM OF SOUNDBOARD AND BASEBOARD

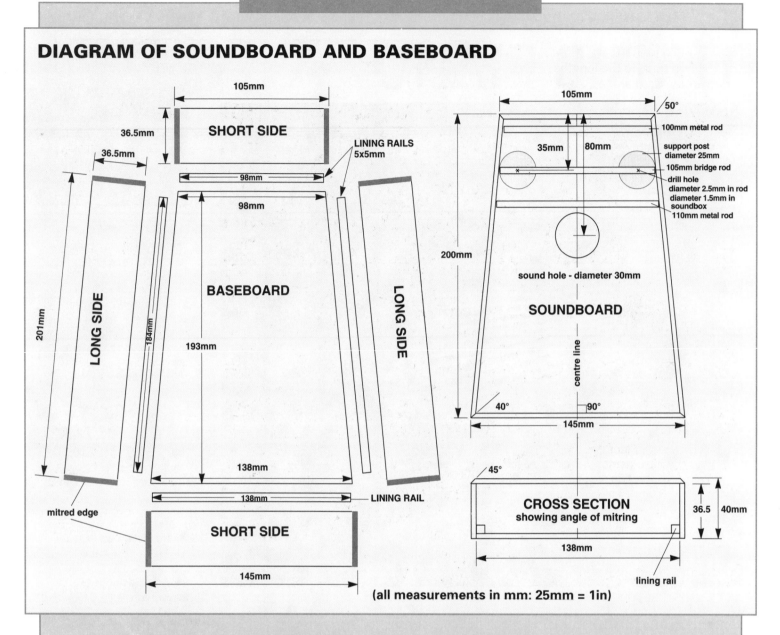

105mm

SHORT SIDE

36.5mm

36.5mm

98mm

LINING RAILS
5x5mm

98mm

201mm

LONG SIDE

184mm

BASEBOARD

193mm

LONG SIDE

138mm

mitred edge

138mm — LINING RAIL

SHORT SIDE

145mm

105mm /50°

100mm metal rod

35mm   80mm

support post
diameter 25mm

105mm bridge rod

drill hole
diameter 2.5mm in rod
diameter 1.5mm in
soundbox

110mm metal rod

200mm

sound hole - diameter 30mm

SOUNDBOARD

centre line

40°   90°

145mm

45°

CROSS SECTION
showing angle of mitring

36.5   40mm

138mm

lining rail

(all measurements in mm: 25mm = 1in)

1 Using an HB pencil and a metal ruler, draw up the dimensions of the baseboard, sides and soundboard on the hardwood. Fix the sawing platform (see wooden jigsaw) to the edge of the work surface with a G-clamp. Using a fretsaw, cut all the pieces along your ruled outlines, cutting outside the line rather than inside. Place the soundboard on the shooting board and plane the edges at a 90° angle to the correct measurements. Then do the same with the sides and the baseboard.

2 Cut the wooden rod into four lining rails, to the lengths shown on the diagram, and glue them on to the inside edge of the baseboard. Use clothes pegs strengthened with rubber bands to clamp the lining rails in position. Leave to dry for two hours.

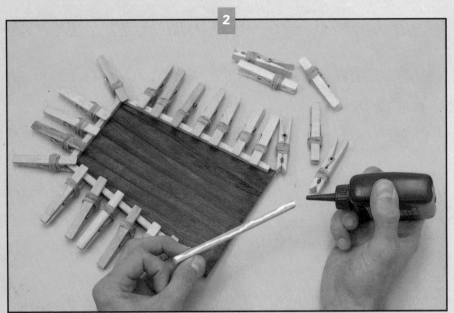

3 Use a pencil to mark the shaded areas to mitre on the side pieces so that they fit together (see diagram). Place the sides on an anvil and mitre using a rasp. Plane the sides of the baseboard again to ensure a smooth edge.

4 Position the sides around the baseboard and check that there are no gaps showing. Apply glue to the bottom inside edge of each side. Glue the sides to the lining rails and wrap 10m (11yds) of tape tightly around the sides to hold them firmly in position. Fix the end of the tape to one side with a peg.

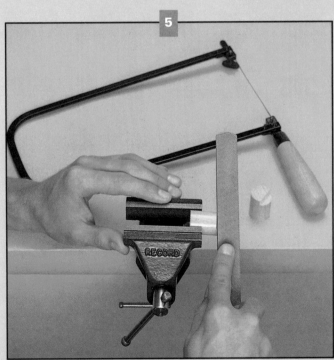

5 While the glue is drying use the broom handle to make two soundboard support posts. Put the broom handle in the vice and cut off two pieces each 33mm (1¼in) long. Cut a segment 5mm (³/₁₆in) wide and 5mm (³/₁₆in) deep off the bottom of each post as shown, using the fretsaw. This is to enable them to fit over the lining rails. Then rasp the ends of each post.

6 Mark the positions of the soundboard posts on the baseboard, and then glue the posts to the baseboard making sure they are as close as possible to the sides of the box. Clamp the posts in position and leave the glue to dry for two hours.

7 Draw the centre line on the soundboard with a pencil. Measure 8cm (3$\frac{1}{8}$in) from the top of the soundboard and draw the sounding hole with a compass, with a radius of 15mm ($\frac{5}{8}$in).

8 Attach the 2mm ($\frac{1}{16}$in) drill bit to the hand drill. Drill a starter hole into the sound hole to thread the fretsaw blade through. Clamp the sawing platform firmly to the table and cut out the sound hole with the fretsaw. Smooth the edges with a rasp.

9 Once the glue has dried on the baseboard, use the plane to level off the top of the soundboard support posts with the sides.

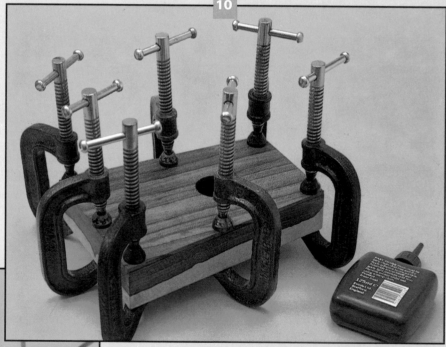

10 Check that the soundboard fits, then glue it on to the top of the box. Use clamps to hold the soundboard in position, and leave to dry.

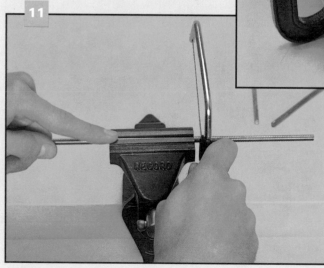

11 Next cut the three metal rods that will support the keys. The rods measure 100mm (3$\frac{15}{16}$in), 105mm (4$\frac{1}{8}$in) and 110mm (4$\frac{11}{32}$in). Mark these measurements on a 35cm (13$\frac{3}{4}$in) metal rod and put the rod in the vice. Cut the rods to their length with the metal saw and smooth off the ends with the metal file. Polish with wire wool.

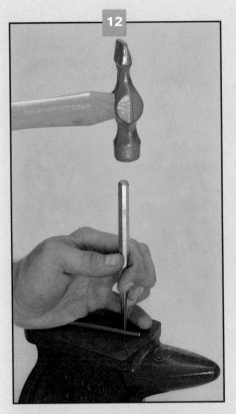

12 Select the 105mm (4¹/₈in) metal rod that will hold down the keys. Place on the anvil and hammer the centre punch 12.5mm (¹/₂in) from each end to mark where you want to drill two holes.

13 Clamp the rod in the vice and drill the holes using the 3mm (¹/₈in) drill bit. Using the fretsaw cut out a strip of hardwood 105 x 10mm (4¹/₈ x ³/₈in). Position the rod over the wooden strip and mark two holes in the wood to line up with the holes in the metal rod. Using the 3mm (¹/₈in) drill bit, drill the holes in the wood. Check that the two 2.5 x 30mm (¹/₈in x 1³/₁₆in) screws fit the holes in both the rod and the wooden strip. This wooden strip will go between the metal rod and the keys to create the 'bridge' on the soundboard.

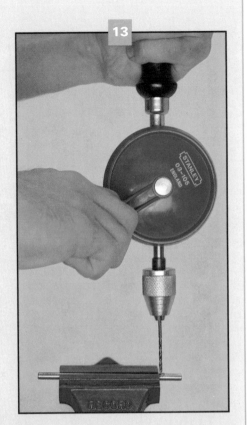

14 Cut the remaining metal rods to the following lengths: 2 x 11.5cm (4¹/₂in), 2 x 12cm (4³/₄in), 2 x 12.5cm (5in), 2 x 13.5cm (5⁵/₁₆in), 2 x 14cm (5¹/₂in), 2 x 14.5cm (5¹¹/₁₆in) (these include 1cm (³/₈in) extra for tuning). Hammer one end of each rod flat on the anvil.

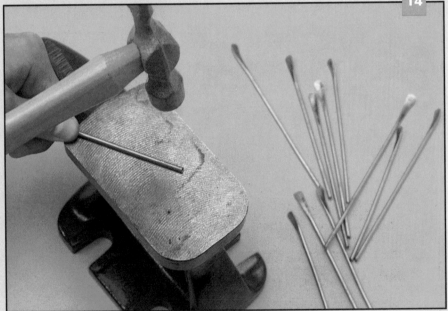

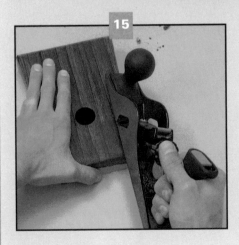

15 For a more comfortable grip on the thumb piano, plane off the edges of the soundboard at an angle of 45°.

16 Using the metal bridge rod as a guide, mark two holes in the soundboard 35mm (1³/₈in) from the top, and drill with the 2mm (¹/₁₆in) drill bit.

17 Clean up the soundbox with the scraper and sandpaper, then apply the wax with wire wool. Wax the soundbox several times, following the grain of the wood. The wax will protect your soundbox and give a more natural shine to the wood.

TUNING

Tune your instrument by adjusting the length of the keys from the bridge. The long keys produce low notes and the shorter keys high ones. The keys are often tuned to only five, six or seven notes, so two keys may give the same note, perhaps at different pitches. Play around by ear until you find a tuning that suits you. Once tuning is complete you can tighten up the bridge and saw off the uneven ends.

18 Attach the rod and wooden strip to the soundboard with the two 2.5 x 30mm ($1/8$ x $1^3/16$in) screws. Position the remaining two round ended rods on the soundboard (see diagram). Sort out your keys in order of length. Thread the longest key under the bridge, and rest it on the two round-ended rods. Secure it in the centre of the soundboard by tightening the bridge slightly with

the screws. Make sure that you don't tighten the bridge too much at this stage or you won't be able to insert the other keys. Insert the other keys, one at a time, so that the shortest keys are on the outside. When all the keys are inserted, tighten the bridge to hold them in place.

Fitting the keys requires patience. The notes will sound louder once you have trimmed the ends. We have used 12 keys, but you can use as many as will fit your thumb piano. Make sure that the ends of the keys don't touch each other as this will produce a different tone. It is also a good idea to bend the flat ends of the keys slightly upwards so that the thumb or forefinger has a better grip.

SCULPTURE AND 3-D

PICTURE FRAMING

MATERIALS

To make the project framed picture you will need:

Above, picture; ready-cut window mount; tape measure; pencil; mitre block; tenon saw; rebated moulding; 4 corner clamps; PVA wood glue; wood filler.

Above, water-soluble powdered pigment stain; jam jar; teaspoon; 25mm (1in) decorator's brush; polyurethane gloss varnish; white spirit; picture-framing glass; glass-cleaning fluid; cloth; sheet of hardboard; fine sandpaper; panel pins; brown gummed tape; craft knife; bradawl; 2 screw eyes; picture string.

You have already learned basic woodworking techniques in earlier projects such as the weather vane and the African thumb piano. Now we put these skills to use in the craft of picture framing, and show you how to frame your own work.

It was not until the 15th century, when painters came to be regarded as artists in their own right rather than simply the servants of powerful patrons, that frames began to be used to set paintings apart from their surroundings. Today, picture framing can be an expensive business. In our project we show you how for a modest outlay you can achieve professional results when framing your own paintings and prints.

A frame should draw attention to the picture without dominating it, so choose your moulding with care. In this project we have framed a watercolour, using a ready-cut mount (which will keep the glass off the surface of the painting) and a simple rebated moulding (the rebate allows for the glass and backing board to be fitted). Decide on the size of the mount first and calculate the required length of moulding

from this (see next page). Once you have assembled the frame you can have the glass and hardboard backing board cut to size.

Accuracy in cutting the 45° mitred corners is all-important, and it follows that the more you spend on a mitre block, the better the results. The widely available wooden mitre block (which looks rather like a three-sided box) is adequate, but the metal mitre block that we have used is worth investing in if you intend to do a lot of framing. There is a wide variety of mouldings available, but we suggest that you start with one with a simple profile and a width of about 4cm (1³/₄in). Buying a plain wood or synthetic 'wood' moulding will give you scope to add your own finish to the frame. We have used a water-soluble powdered pigment stain to colour the frame, plus a coat of glossy varnish.

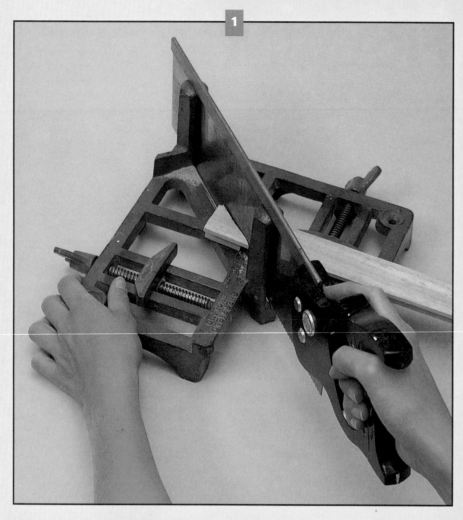

To calculate the length of moulding you need to buy, measure the four edges of the mount. To allow for the mitred corners, measure the width of your chosen moulding and multiply this by eight. Add the two figures together and add an extra 10cm (4in) for safety.

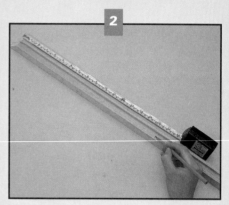

2 Take the measurement of one side of the mount, adding 1cm ($^3/_8$in) to the length (this will allow 5mm ($^3/_{16}$in) fitting space on either side of the mount). Remove the moulding from the mitre block and mark the measurement in pencil on the lower edge of the rebate.

1 Have a window mount with a bevelled edge professionally cut for your picture and estimate the length of moulding you require (see Helpful Hint, *above*). Secure one end of the moulding in the mitre block and saw it off, to give a 45° mitred end for the first piece of the frame.

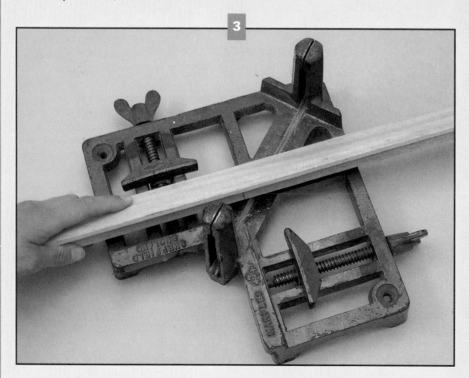

When cutting the moulding make sure that you cut at the correct angle. The edge with the rebate (the inside edge of the frame) is always the shortest.

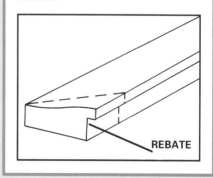

REBATE

3 Place the moulding in the mitre block (on the opposite side to step 1), aligning the pencil mark with the centre of the cutting groove of the block.

4 Secure the moulding in the mitre block and cut it with the saw. Remove the moulding and put this first cut piece to one side.

5 Place the remaining length of moulding in the other side of the mitre block and cut off the end to give a mitred cut for one end of the second piece. Remove the moulding.

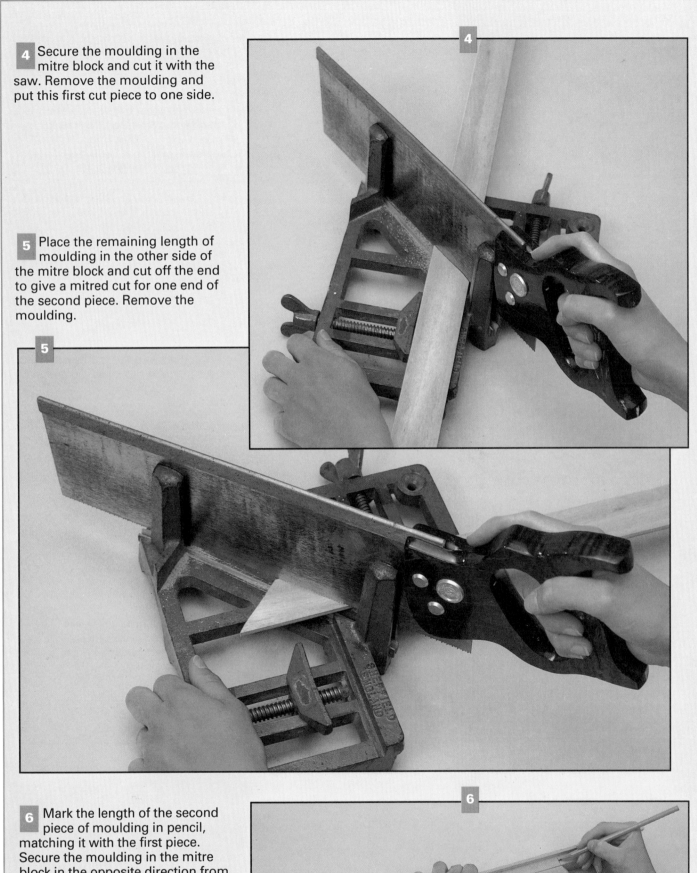

6 Mark the length of the second piece of moulding in pencil, matching it with the first piece. Secure the moulding in the mitre block in the opposite direction from step 5 and cut. Repeat step 5 to make a mitred cut for the third piece. Cut the remaining pieces of moulding, following the instructions from step 2, taking the measurement from the other side of the window mount.

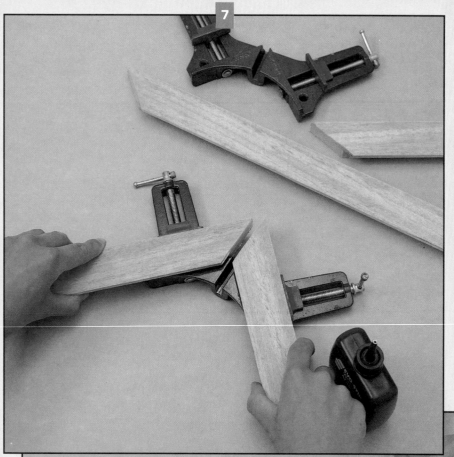

HELPFUL HINT

Lay out the pieces of moulding for the frame in position so that you are sure to assemble the frame in the correct order.

7 Secure one piece of moulding in a corner clamp, lining up the mitred corner with the centre of the groove. Apply glue generously to the corresponding end of the second piece, slide into place and secure. Wipe off the excess glue with a damp cloth. Secure the free end of one of these pieces in a corner clamp and glue the third piece in place. Secure the two free ends in two corner clamps; apply glue to both ends of the fourth piece, place in position and secure in the corner clamps. Wipe off the excess glue.

8 Leave the glue to dry for about 2 hours. Tidy up the joins at the corners by applying wood filler with your finger. Smooth down, and wipe off any excess with a damp cloth. Remove the clamps.

9 Mix ½ a teaspoon of powdered pigment stain in a small quantity of water and test the colour on a scrap of moulding. Apply the stain to the frame with a decorator's brush. Leave to dry.

10 Apply a coat of varnish to the frame. Leave to dry. Clean the brush with white spirit.

11 Take the measurement for the glass and the hardboard from the rebate, less 2mm ($^1/_{16}$in) on all sides, and have them cut to size. Position the picture behind the mount, temporarily attaching it with masking tape, and then secure with brown gummed tape along the top edge. Remove the masking tape. Clean the glass with cleaning fluid and a cloth. Place the frame face down, and place the glass in position on the moulding. Place the mount and the picture on the glass, then place the hardboard in position.

12 Tap the panel pins halfway into the frame at 8cm (3in) intervals with the hammer, then gently tap the projecting part of the pin down onto the surface of the hardboard to hold it in place.

13 Cut strips of brown gummed tape, moisten with a wet cloth, and glue in position to seal the join. Apply a second layer of tape.

14 Mark a point on each side of the back of the frame one third of the way down from the top. Make a starter hole with the bradawl and screw in a screw eye on each side. Tie a length of picture string securely to the screw eyes.

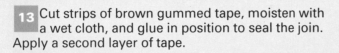

The colour of the frame should reflect, or contrast with, the colour of the painting. A colour stain allows the grain to show through. It can be left untreated, given a coat of gloss varnish, or rubbed with wax to further accentuate the grain. If you prefer the look of natural wood, protect it with a coat of varnish or wax. Alternatively, paint the frame with acrylic paint.

SCULPTURE AND 3-D

WOODEN CACTI

MATERIALS

To make the sculpture shown *below left* you will need:

Above, 20cm (8in) of 2 x 1in softwood; 30cm (12in) of 3 x 1in softwood; 25cm (10in) of 2in round softwood; 60cm (24in) of $^1/_4$in dowel; 200 zinc-plated half-round Pozidriv self-tapping screws 6 x $^3/_8$in; steel panel pins 20 x 1.6mm ($^3/_4$ x $^1/_{16}$in); steel panel pins 30 x 1.6mm (1$^3/_{16}$ x $^1/_{16}$in); 8 red wire-ended miniature light-emitting diodes; terracotta flowerpot; 2kg (4$^1/_2$lb) plaster of Paris; polythene bag; yellow sand.

Above, vice; electric jigsaw; mini drill; hand drill; drill bits, $^1/_{16}$in, $^7/_{64}$in, $^1/_4$in; Pozidriv screwdriver; $^1/_4$in wood-carving gouge; hammer; wood glue; ruler; pencil; carbon paper; masking tape.

This woodworking project takes standard wood off-cuts and fashions them with mechanical and hand tools to produce a witty sculpture of petrified cacti — coloured with inks and studded with nails, screws and mini electronic components.

Above, green, yellow and blue waterproof drawing ink; 15mm ($^3/_4$in) flat paintbrush; mixing dish; newsprint; stiff card 100 x 300mm (4 x 12in); bright green car spray paint; craft knife; PVA wood glue; plastic bucket; 12mm ($^1/_2$in) decorator's brush; old spoon.

Cacti make good models for sculpture. They have easily recognisable features, such as the method of branching used in the larger cactus in the project, and if you study living specimens closely, you will see that the spines of each variety are arranged in a precise, regular pattern.

Materials and equipment

We use an electric jigsaw to shape the pieces initially (although you could use a hand saw) and then the final shaping and texturing is done with a wood-carving gouge. The pattern of spines on the plants is reproduced with screws and nails, and flowers are suggested with red light-emitting diodes.

You can obtain the timber, screws and nails from a builder's merchant. The electric jigsaw is rather expensive, but you could probably hire one for the project. If you own an electric drill, you won't need the mini-drill and the hand drill. The LEDs (light-emitting diodes) can be bought at an electronic components shop.

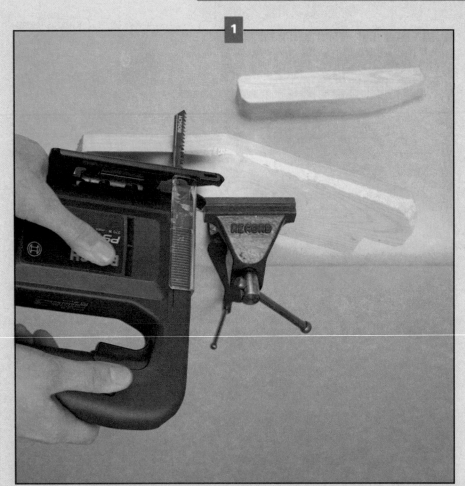

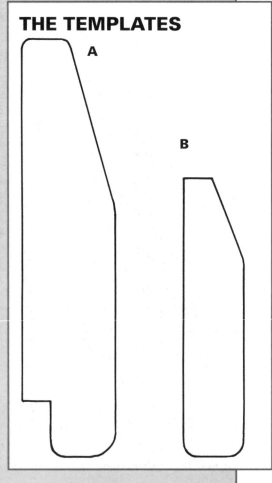

THE TEMPLATES

A

B

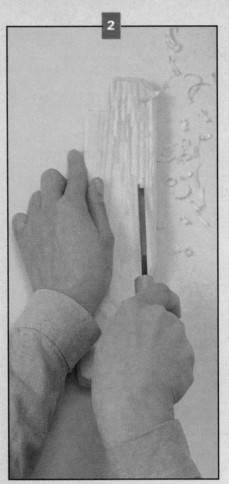

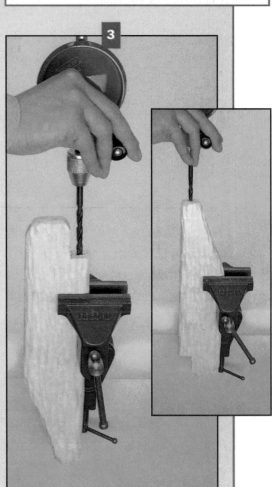

1 Enlarge the templates on a photocopier at 200%, then again at 135%. Transfer template **A** to the 3 x 1-inch piece of wood using carbon paper. Transfer template **B** to the 2 x 1-inch piece of wood. Clamp each piece of wood in a vice and cut out the shapes with a jigsaw, then round off all the corners.

SAFETY FIRST
When using the jigsaw, follow the manufacturer's instructions carefully and always keep the safety shield in place.

2 With the gouge, finish shaping the edges and texture the flat surfaces of the wood by gouging out short lengths.

3 Clamp piece A upright in the vice. Using the mini drill and a 7/64-inch bit, drill a small hole in the centre of the step, then enlarge it to about 5cm (2in) deep using the hand drill and a 1/4-inch bit. Invert the wood and drill a hole the same size in the base (see inset).

4 Drill another hole the same size in the centre of the narrow end of piece B. Push one end of the dowel into the hole in the step of piece A and use a pencil to mark the depth of the hole. Measure the depth of the hole in piece B in the same way. Add the two measurements together and cut a piece of dowel to that length using a craft knife (roll the dowel as you cut it — this makes the job easier).

5 Squeeze wood glue into each hole. Insert one end of the dowel into the hole in piece A, then slip piece B over the other end so that the two pieces are joined. Piece B should stand at right angles to piece A.

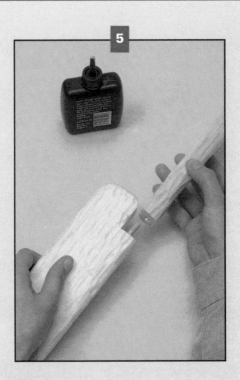

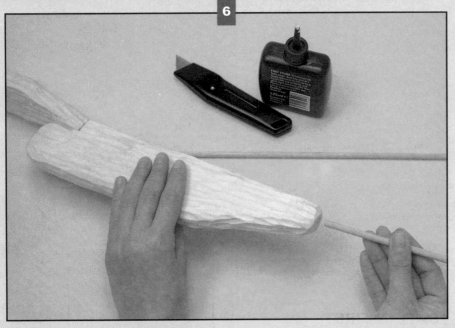

6 Squeeze wood glue into the hole in the narrow end of piece A. Cut a 15cm (6in) length of dowel and insert one end into the hole.

7 Construct the other cactus from the piece of 2-inch round softwood in the same way as before: cut the wood to 25cm (10in), round off all the corners with a jigsaw and shape and texture with a gouge. Finally drill a 1/4-inch hole in the base and glue in a 15cm (6in) length of dowel.

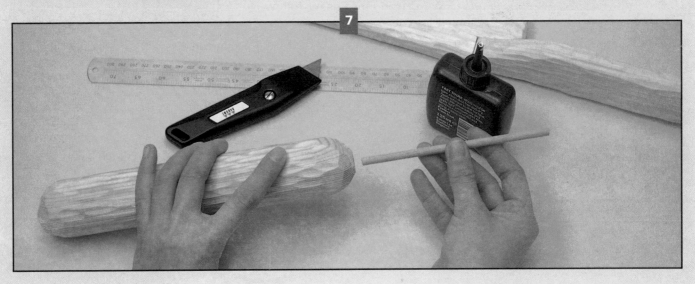

8 In a bowl mix green and blue inks in the proportion 1:2 (mix plenty of ink so that you don't run out halfway). Paint the first cactus all over and leave it to dry. Mix yellow and green inks in the proportion 5:1, and use this to paint the round cactus.

9 When both pieces are thoroughly dry lay them on a sheet of newsprint and spray them lightly with the green car spray, leaving the base colours showing through in places (do this in a well-ventilated room, or outdoors, as the fumes are quite strong).

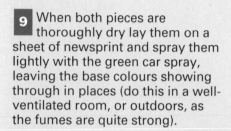

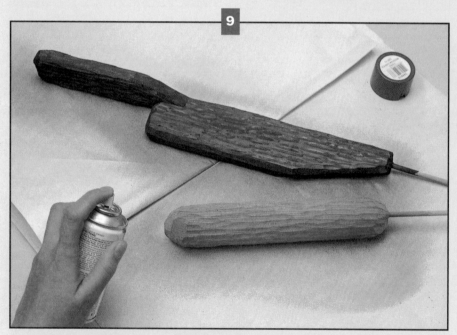

10 When dry, use the mini drill and the $7/64$-inch bit to drill a series of shallow holes 2.5cm (1in) apart, in a pattern of diagonal lines, all over the first cactus, including the narrow sides. Avoid drilling holes exactly opposite each other on the two flat surfaces otherwise when the screws are inserted they will hit each other.

11 Using the screwdriver, screw a screw into each hole so that the head is firmly in contact with the surface of the wood.

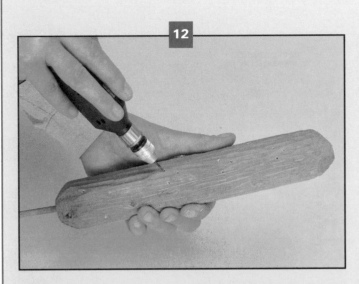

12 On the round cactus, drill groups of three holes all over the surface using the $^1/_{16}$-inch bit. The holes in each group should be about 8mm ($^5/_{16}$in) apart, and the groups about 30mm (1in) apart. Drill the holes at roughly 45°, the upper ones angled downwards and the lower ones upwards. On the top, drill a hole in the centre and three holes around it.

13 Hammer a long panel pin into the top hole of each group of three, and two short pins into the lower ones.

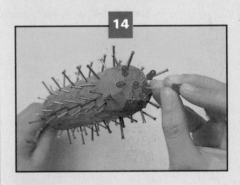

14 Push two red light-emitting diodes into each of the holes at the top of the cactus to form the flower.

15 With a craft knife, score two lines across the width of the card, each 12cm (4$^3/_4$in) from an end. Turn the card over and score two more lines, 10cm (4in) from the ends. Bend along the score lines and fit the card into the flower pot to form a 'bridge' 2cm ($^3/_4$in) below the rim. Position the cacti where you want them and make two holes in the card for the stalks.

HELPFUL HINT

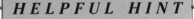

Make sure you buy a good-quality, frost-resistant terracotta pot — cheap pots sometimes crack due to the pressure exerted by the plaster of Paris.

16 Remove the card bridge. Cut along one side of the plastic bag, open it out and line the flower pot with it. In a bucket, mix plaster of Paris with two pints of water and fill the flower pot to within 2cm (³/₄in) of the rim.

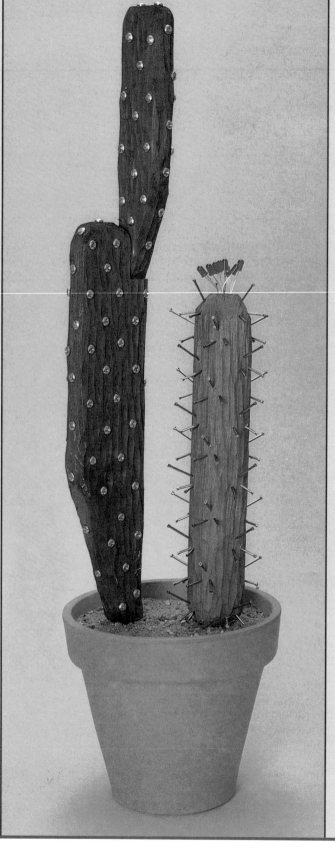

17 Push the card bridge into the top of the pot and push the stalks of the cacti through the holes into the wet plaster, making sure they are standing straight. Leave for at least two hours for the plaster to harden fully.

18 Remove the card and trim away any surplus plastic. Coat the surface of the plaster with PVA wood glue, then sprinkle a layer of sand over it while still wet.

You could visit a garden centre to study the shapes of different types of cactus 'in the flesh'. Then design your own cactus sculpture using the methods shown in this project. These cacti look particularly effective arranged in groups of three or more, in a variety of shapes and sizes.

SCULPTURE AND 3-D

JACOB'S LADDER

In this project we show you how to make a traditional toy called a Jacob's Ladder. The toy is easily made from blocks of wood, lengths of gift ribbon and some self-adhesive labels, and is guaranteed to baffle and amaze your friends.

The Jacob's Ladder was a popular folk-toy during the late 19th century, and children still play with it today. The toy uses an ancient principle originally used in a Chinese conjuring trick, but it takes its name from the Bible — in the *Book of Genesis* there is an account of a dream of the prophet Jacob, in which he sees a ladder extending from earth to heaven on which the angels ascend and descend.

Magic patterns
The design of the Jacob's Ladder is very simple, consisting of a chain of thin wooden blocks which are connected to one another by strips of ribbon of different colours. The way in which the ribbons are attached to the wooden blocks is ingeniously designed to create the illusion of the blocks tumbling

or falling over one another when the toy is used. Even more ingeniously, the patterns on the ribbons magically change as the blocks tumble.

Tumble action
In order to work the Jacob's Ladder, hold the chain of blocks vertically in the air so that one of the patterns is visible. Hold the top block by the edges and tip it forward (or back) so that it touches the second block. This triggers the tumbling action of the other blocks, and as they tumble the pattern changes as if by magic.

Making the Jacob's Ladder can be fiddly until you get into the rhythm of it; before you start it is advisable to study the diagrams overleaf and practise with some spare blocks of wood and pieces of ribbon.

MATERIALS

To make the Jacob's Ladder shown *below left* you will need:

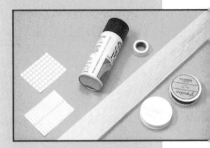

Above, length of softwood such as pine, 10mm (³/₈in) thick and at least 60cm (24in) long and 65mm (2¹/₂in) wide; spool each of black and white gift ribbon, 19mm (³/₄in) wide; double-sided tape, 15mm (⁵/₈in) wide; white 8mm (⁵/₁₆in) round self-adhesive labels; white rectangular self-adhesive labels, 35mm x 5mm (1¹/₂ x ¹/₄in); can of black spray paint.

Above, coping saw and medium blade; G-clamp; vice; plane; sanding block, medium grade; metal ruler; pencil; scissors; two small wood offcuts; newsprint.

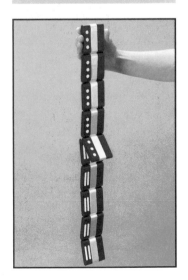

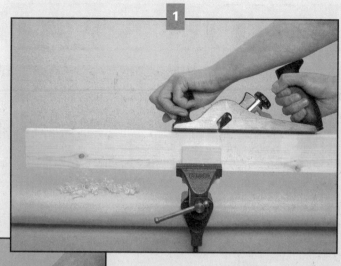

1 Clamp the piece of timber to the work bench and cut it to a length of 600mm (23⁵/₈in) and width of 65mm (2⁹/₁₆in) with the coping saw. Fix the timber in the jaws of the vice as shown, with a small wood offcut either side to protect it. Holding the plane at a slight angle, round off the sharp edges on the long sides of the wood. Smooth with the sanding block.

2 With a ruler and pencil, mark off the length of wood at 6cm (2³/₈in) intervals. Clamp the wood to the work bench, protecting it from marks with the offcuts. Cut out all the 'squares' with the coping saw (the 'squares' actually measure 6 x 6.5cm/2³/₈ x2⁹/₁₆in).

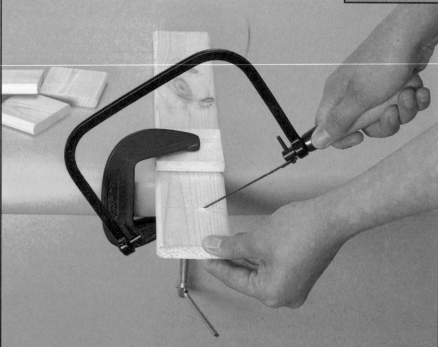

3 Smooth all the cut edges of the squares with the sanding block.

4 Working outdoors, place all the squares on a sheet of newsprint and spray them with black paint. When they are dry, turn them over and spray the other side. Leave to dry.

5 Take one of the squares and wrap three strips of double-sided tape around it lengthways, as shown; start with the two outer strips, placing them close to the edges, then apply the central strip. Repeat for the remaining squares.

6 Cut the white gift ribbon into seven 26cm (10in) lengths and two 33cm (13in) lengths. Cut the black ribbon into fourteen 26cm (10in) and four 33cm (13in) lengths.

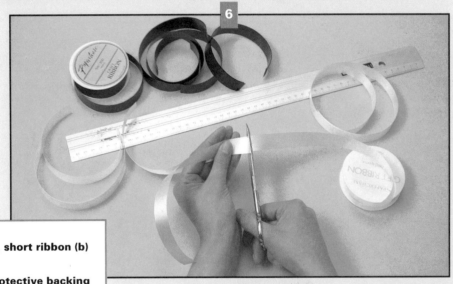

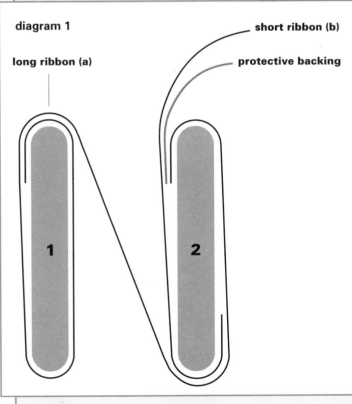

diagram 1

long ribbon (a)

short ribbon (b)

protective backing

1

2

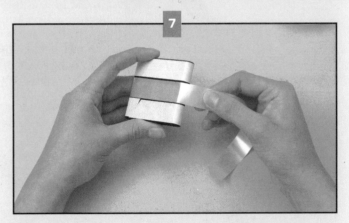

7 Take the first square and remove the backing paper from the middle strip of tape. Following diagram **1**, begin attaching the white ribbons: take one of the long lengths of white ribbon, **a**, and stick down one end about 1.5cm (⅝in) in from the edge of the square, then wrap it round the square — there should be about 9cm (3½in) of ribbon left free at the end.

8 Again following diagram **1**, repeat for the second square, but this time use a short length of ribbon, **b**. When you remove the backing paper from the tape, stick down one end of it 1.5cm (⁵/₈in) in from the opposite edge on the reverse side of the square from where you began sticking down the ribbon. Continue wrapping the ribbon around the square.

9 Now place square 2 on top of square 1 so that the loose end of the long ribbon is sandwiched between the two. Bring the end of ribbon **a** up over the top of square 2 and tuck it in behind the piece of backing paper. Remove the backing paper.

10 Following diagram **2**, repeat using short lengths of ribbon, for the next six squares. The photograph shows how the puzzle should look at this stage. Attach the remaining long ribbon to square 9, as shown in diagram **2**, then secure the last short ribbon before attaching the end of the long ribbon to square 10.

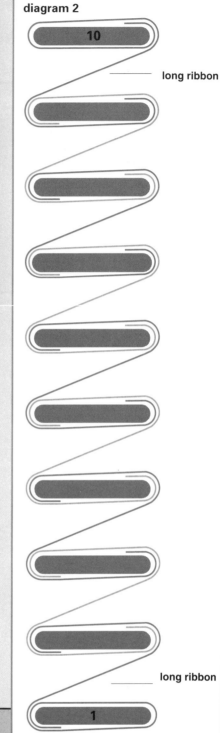

diagram 2

long ribbon

long ribbon

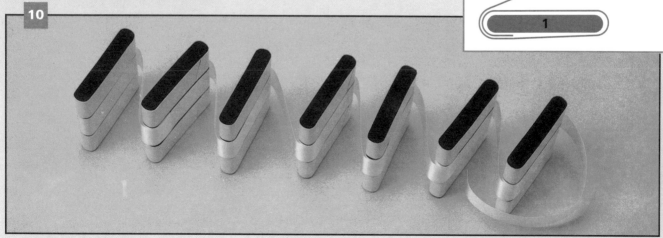

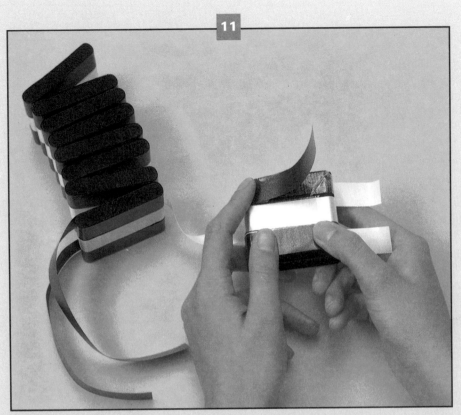

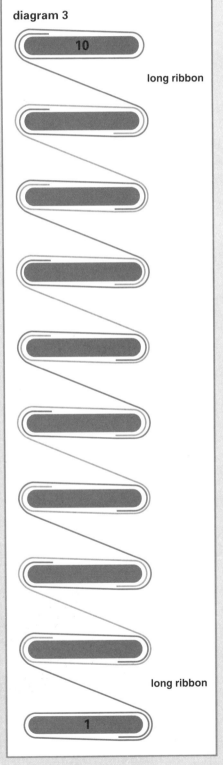

11 Starting with square 1, begin attaching the black ribbons either side of the white ribbon. As before, attach the long ribbons between squares 1 and 2, and 9 and 10. Use diagram **3** as a guide for the positioning of the ribbons.

diagram 3

10

long ribbon

long ribbon

1

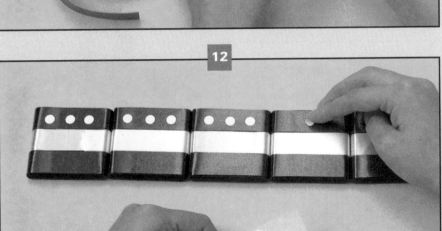

12 Open the ladder out and lay it flat on the work surface. Stick a row of three round self-adhesive labels on each square along one side of the ladder only.

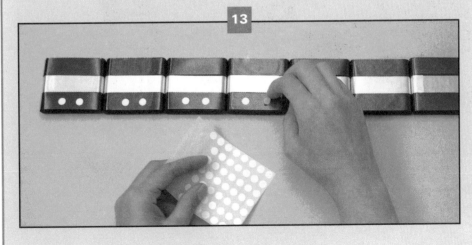

13 Turn the ladder over and stick two round self-adhesive labels on each square, as shown.

14 Pick up the ladder and hold it vertically so that you can see the row of three-dot squares. Hold the top square by the edges and tip it back to touch the second square; the blocks will tumble to reveal a row of blank squares. Now place the ladder flat again, blank squares upwards. Stick two rectangular self-adhesive labels to each square, along one edge only.

15 Turn the ladder over. There should be three white circles on each end square. Trim 24 rectangular self-adhesive labels to 1.5cm (^{5}/8in) and stick three to each remaining square between the dots.

HELPFUL HINT

Don't worry if your Jacob's Ladder 'sticks' at first. The ribbons may be a little tight, but they will gradually loosen up as the toy is used.

16 Now close up the ladder so that the square on top tilts backwards and forwards. If the top square will not tilt both ways, open the ladder up and fold it up the other way. Pick up the ladder and hold it vertically. Tilt the top square forwards to trigger the tumbling action of the other squares and reveal a different pattern. Turn the ladder around and repeat the process to reveal another sequence of patterns.

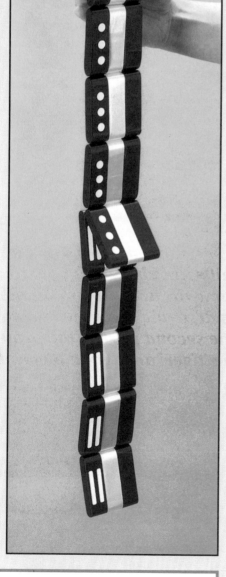

As you play with the Jacob's Ladder the patterns will change again and again. See if your friends can work out the mystery! You can, of course, use coloured ribbons and labels instead of black and white ones.

SCULPTURE AND 3-D

BOARD GAME

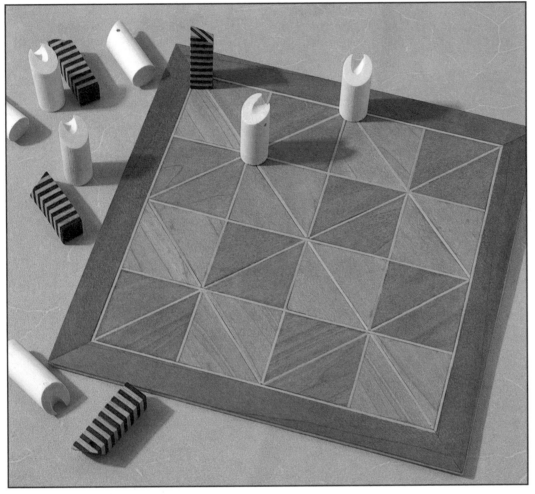

MATERIALS

To make the board game shown *below left* you will need:

Above, four 1m (1yd) lengths of dyed veneer: green, blue, yellow, black; four 1m (1yd) lengths of white boxwood line No. 10; sheet of 1/8in plywood, 270mm (10³/4in) square; 2 pieces of 3/4in MDF, 300mm (12in) square; four 50mm (2in) bolts with wing nuts; four steel 6mm (1/4in) penny washers.

Above, vice; hand drill; 7/32in wood bit; cutting board; fine grade sandpaper; sheet of silicone paper (baking parchment); masking tape; double-sided adhesive tape; craft knife; scissors; metal ruler; pencil; 45° set-square; PVA wood glue; 2 flat 1/2in brushes; jar.

In a double project designed to extend your woodworking skills, we show you how to construct a fascinating board game for two players. In this first part we make the board itself, using a simple marquetry technique with dyed veneer. The second part of the project will be devoted to modelling the 'tiger' and 'goat' pieces with which the game is played.

Our board game is a modern version of a traditional game from Katmandu in Nepal, known there as 'the tiger-moving game'. We will explain the rules of the game in full in the second part of the project, but essentially it is played in a similar way to draughts. The aim of the game is for the tigers to gobble up all the goats, while the goats have to try and corner the tigers.

Materials and construction
The board is made from plywood inlaid with a geometric marquetry pattern (technically known as parquetry) cut from pieces of wafer-thin, dyed veneer and boxwood line. With the exception of some of the materials needed to make the playing pieces, we have listed on this page all the materials you will need for the complete project. The dyed veneers and white boxwood can be obtained from timber merchants and veneer specialists, or a cabinet maker may let you buy his offcuts. The plywood, dowel and other materials are available from builder's merchants. If you own a power drill you won't need the mini-drill or the hand drill, and the electric jigsaw can be hired for this project.

You should allow at least three days to complete the board and pieces — not because they are difficult to make, but because at several stages during their construction they have to be placed in a press or a clamp and left, preferably overnight, for the glue to dry.

HELPFUL HINT

A veneer is a thin layer of wood cut by machine. Expensive and rare woods are cut into thin pieces and then used to face common, cheaper wood. Handle veneers with care, as they are very delicate.

BOARD GRID (the diagram shows one-quarter of the board)

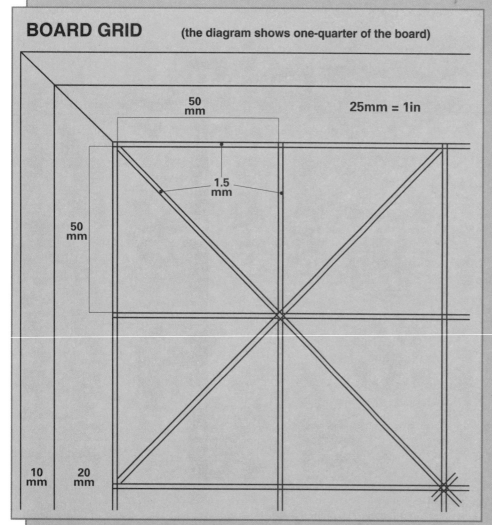

50 mm

25mm = 1in

1.5 mm

50 mm

10 mm

20 mm

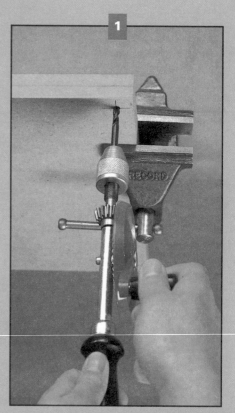

1 Line up the two pieces of MFD board so they are exactly square and clamp them in the vice as shown. Using the hand drill and the $^7/_{32}$-inch bit, drill holes through the two pieces 15mm ($^5/_8$in) from the corners.

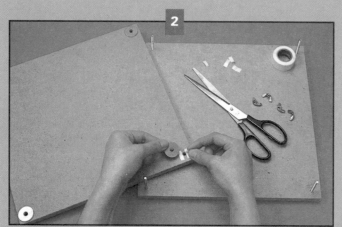

2 To make the press, fit the bolts through the holes in one of the boards, sticking the head of the bolt to the board with double-sided adhesive tape to prevent it dropping off. Stick the $^1/_4$-inch penny washers over the holes in the second piece of board with double-sided tape.

3 Using a pencil and ruler, carefully draw the grid indicated in the diagram on the 270mm (10$^5/_8$in) square piece of $^1/_8$-inch ply. As it must be accurate, don't work from an enlarged photocopy or a tracing, but work directly on to the wood. Use a set square to check that all the squares and diagonals are correct.

TRIANGLE TEMPLATE

Using the set square and lines on the cutting mat as a guide, form a template for cutting the isosceles triangle with strips of masking tape. Apply a double layer for the straight line along the top (the top of the veneer strip aligns with this) and the lefthand side of the triangle. The other strip is the cutting guide. As you cut off each triangle, turn the veneer strip over before making the next cut.

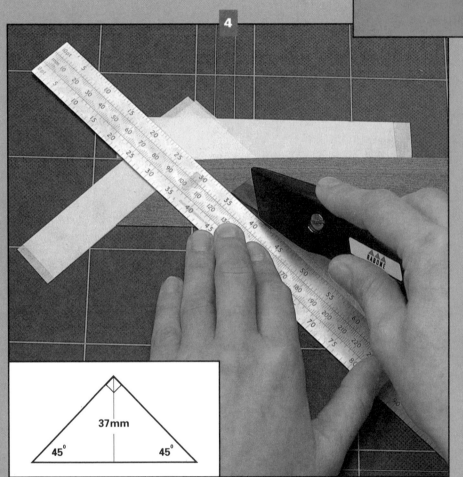

37mm
45° 45°

4 Take the green veneer and cut a strip 37mm (1^{15}/$_{32}$in) wide, following the grain. Using the craft knife and metal ruler, cut the strip into a series of isosceles triangles (with a right angle at the top and 45° angles at the bottom, see diagram inset). You need 32 triangles, plus spares in case any of them break. To make the job easier use a template to cut against (see Triangle template box, *above*).

5 Cut 12 lengths of boxwood line with square ends to exactly 50mm (1^{31}/$_{32}$in). Cut a further 16 lengths with a point at one end to about 75mm (3in) — you will trim the other end once it is glued to the board.

HELPFUL HINT

When gluing the triangles to the board you may find that they tend to curl up, particularly if you are working in a dry atmosphere. To prevent this, lightly dampen the upper side of the triangle before gluing it in place. When laying the squares, you will notice that the grain of the veneer runs diagonally. You can enhance the beauty of the marquetry pattern by laying the squares with the grain running in alternate directions; as the light catches them, they create a chequerboard pattern of light and dark.

6 Start laying out the board at one of the corners. With a clean brush, dampen one side of a green triangle very lightly to prevent it curling up. Paint the first square with PVA wood glue right up to the edges and position the triangle, dry side down. If necessary, trim the edges of the triangle to match the grid exactly.

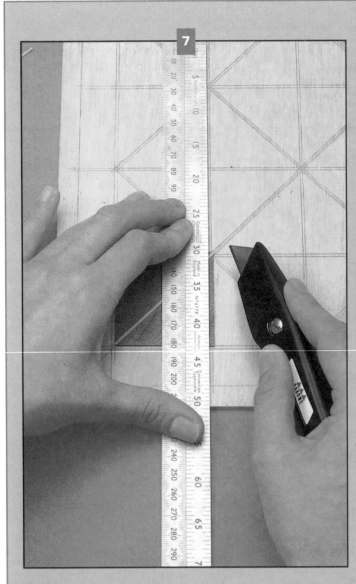

7 Working quickly before the glue has time to dry, lay one of the longer boxwood strips in place with its pointed end fitting into the outer corner of the square. Then lay another triangle. Trim the square so that it lines up perfectly with the righthand line of the grid.

8 Paint PVA wood glue on the next square along. Lay down a short boxwood strip as shown, then complete the square as described in steps 6 and 7. Continue in this way until you reach the end of the first row, finishing with a green triangle.

9 Trim the row you have just laid to fit the line of the grid and peel off the trimmings. At this stage you may find some of the pieces beginning to curl up; so long as they are in the correct position and are not overlapping each other, don't worry.

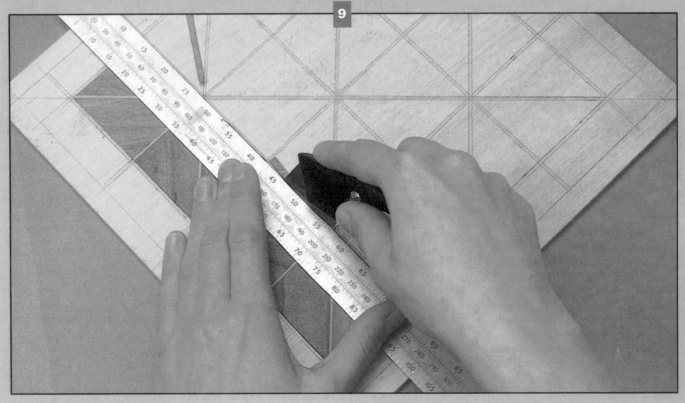

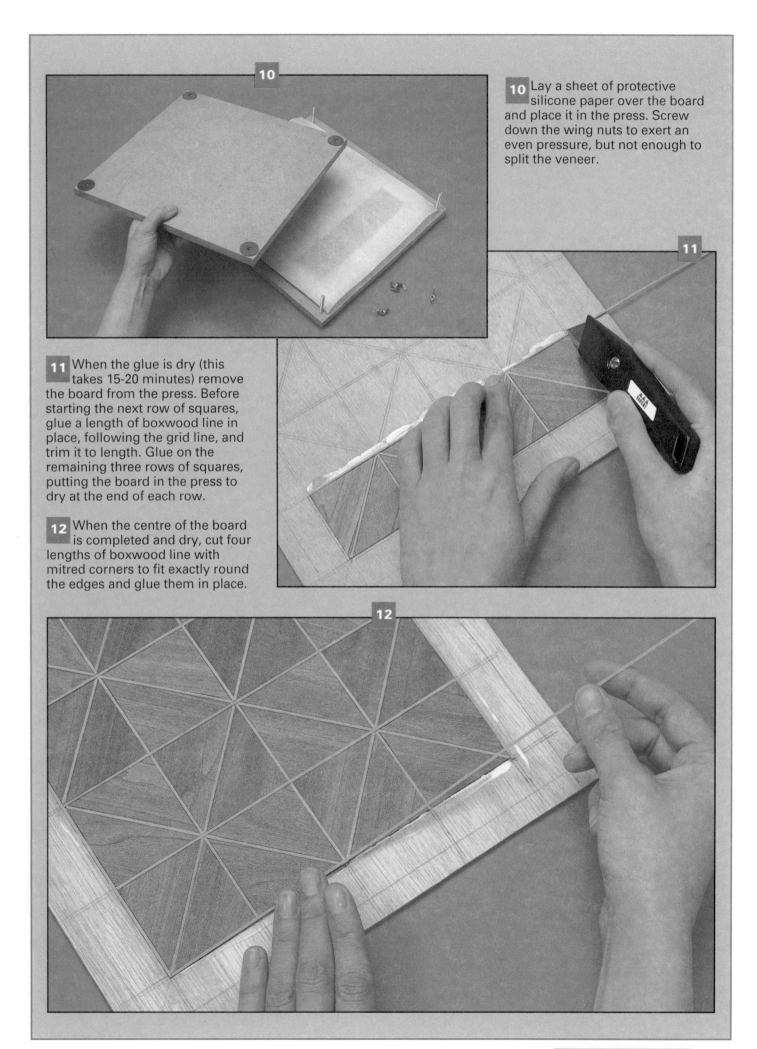

10 Lay a sheet of protective silicone paper over the board and place it in the press. Screw down the wing nuts to exert an even pressure, but not enough to split the veneer.

11 When the glue is dry (this takes 15-20 minutes) remove the board from the press. Before starting the next row of squares, glue a length of boxwood line in place, following the grid line, and trim it to length. Glue on the remaining three rows of squares, putting the board in the press to dry at the end of each row.

12 When the centre of the board is completed and dry, cut four lengths of boxwood line with mitred corners to fit exactly round the edges and glue them in place.

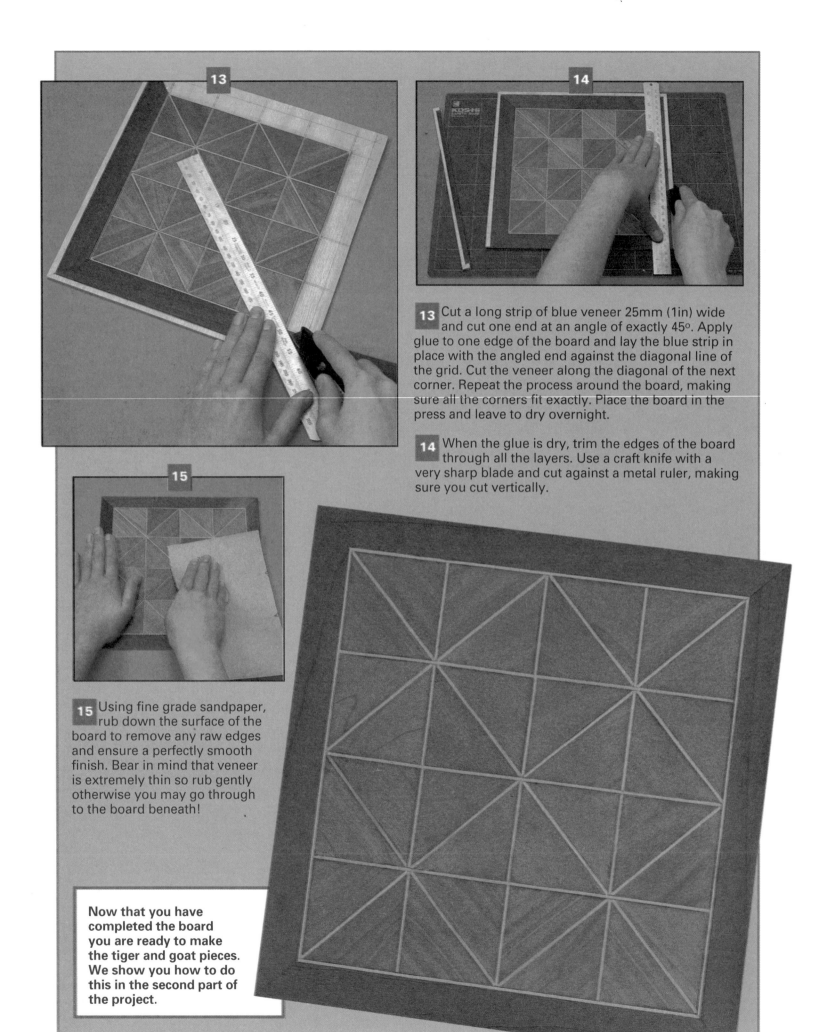

13 Cut a long strip of blue veneer 25mm (1in) wide and cut one end at an angle of exactly 45°. Apply glue to one edge of the board and lay the blue strip in place with the angled end against the diagonal line of the grid. Cut the veneer along the diagonal of the next corner. Repeat the process around the board, making sure all the corners fit exactly. Place the board in the press and leave to dry overnight.

14 When the glue is dry, trim the edges of the board through all the layers. Use a craft knife with a very sharp blade and cut against a metal ruler, making sure you cut vertically.

15 Using fine grade sandpaper, rub down the surface of the board to remove any raw edges and ensure a perfectly smooth finish. Bear in mind that veneer is extremely thin so rub gently otherwise you may go through to the board beneath!

Now that you have completed the board you are ready to make the tiger and goat pieces. We show you how to do this in the second part of the project.

GAME PIECES

MATERIALS

To make the playing pieces shown *below* you will need:

In the second part of our board game project we show you how to make the goat and tiger playing pieces and explain the rules to enable you to play the game.

The tiger pieces are made with the same coloured veneers that were used for the board, but in a slightly unorthodox fashion. Each of the stripes on the pieces is made from five layers of veneer; because the veneers are dyed all the way through, as opposed to being stained on the surface only, the pieces retain their colour even when cut and sanded.

The goat pieces are made in a less labour-intensive way as there are many more of them. Their design exploits the fact that interesting shapes result when holes and straight cuts intersect.

Above, 1m (1yd) of 20mm (³/₄in) dowel; G-clamp with 4in jaws; mini-drill with ⁷/₁₆in bit; ⁵/₁₆in wood bit; fretsaw; jigsaw and metal-cutting blade; piece of 2 x 1in timber as sanding block; ¹/₄in round file; coarse-grade sandpaper; wood bleach and related chemicals; strong plastic bag; rubber gloves.
You will also need the press made in the first part of the project, the board game; strip of yellow veneer; strip of black veneer; vice; hand drill; metal ruler; sharp pencil; craft knife; cutting board; masking tape; PVA wood glue; fine-grade sandpaper; silicone paper (baking parchment).

How to play the 'Goats and tigers' game

The game is played by two players, a tiger-player (who has 4 tigers) and a goat-player (who has 20 goats). It is unusual in that the players have different numbers of pieces and the pieces have different moves and objectives.

To start the game, the tiger-player places his four tigers at the four corners of the board. The goat-player places a goat anywhere on the board.

From then on the players play alternate moves. At each move the tiger-player may move one tiger in any direction from a point on the board to the next point along a white line. For his move the goat-player places a new goat anywhere on the board; when all his goats are on the board (and not before) he can move his pieces around in the same way as the tigers.

The object of the game for the tigers is to gobble up all the goats — a tiger can jump over a goat (eat it) if the space on the other side is free. The goat is then removed from the game for good. The goats have to try to corner the tigers so that they cannot move (but they are not allowed to eat the tigers).

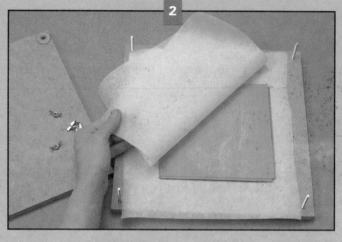

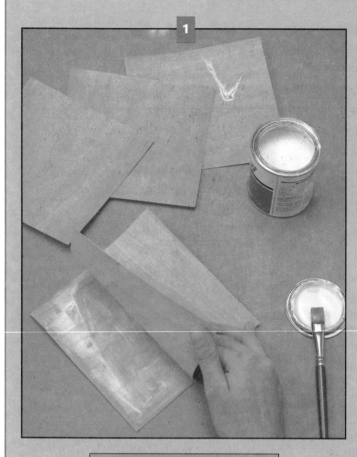

1 To make the tiger pieces, cut the length of yellow veneer into five equal squares. Apply PVA wood glue to one of the squares, making sure the whole surface is covered. Press the second square on to the first with the grain running across the grain of the first.

2 Repeat the process until you have a five-layered sandwich with the grain of the layers alternating in direction. Place the square in the press with a sheet of silicone paper top and bottom (to prevent any squeezed out glue sticking to the press). Leave to dry for several hours. Repeat the whole process with the black veneer.

HELPFUL HINT

When cutting the 15mm (⁵⁄₈in) squares, it is easier to partially cut through the vertical lines first, then cut right through the horizontal lines before finally separating the pieces.

3 Carefully cut the yellow and the black pieces into a series of 15mm (⁵⁄₈in) squares. Use a sharp blade and try to cut the lines perfectly straight or you will have a great deal of sanding to do later. You will need 30 yellow squares and 32 black ones.

4 Take 16 black squares and 15 yellow ones and glue them together to form a column, again with the grain running in alternate directions. Start and finish with a black square.

5 Clamp the column in the G-clamp, applying quite a lot of pressure. Ensure that the column is centred and stays straight. Leave it to dry, preferably overnight, and then repeat the process with the remaining squares.

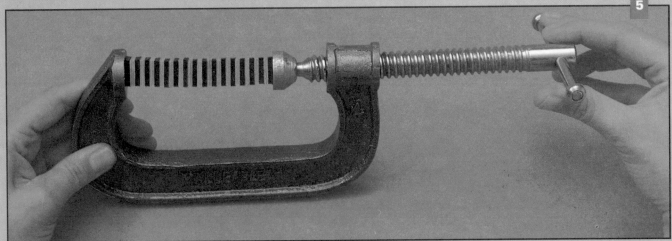

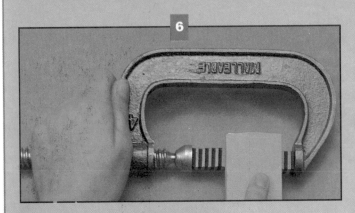

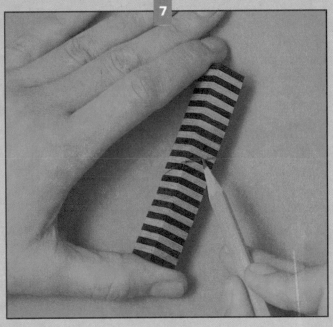

6 For ease of handling, place each column in the clamp in turn and sand each side completely smooth with the sanding block; start with the coarse-grade sandpaper and finish with the fine grade.

7 Halfway along one column, make a pencil mark on a corner edge. Hold the column at an angle so that two surfaces are visible. Using the pencil mark as the centre point, draw a visually straight line diagonally across the two visible faces (see diagram 1). Repeat for the second column.

diagram 1

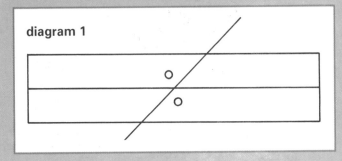

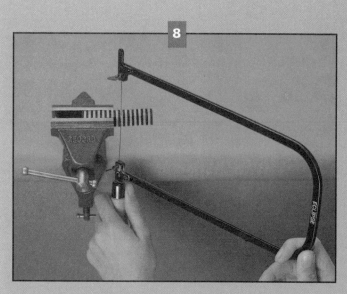

8 Fix each column in the vice and cut it in two along the pencil line using the fretsaw.

9 Sand the diamond-shaped faces of the tigers smooth by rubbing them across a sheet of fine sandpaper.

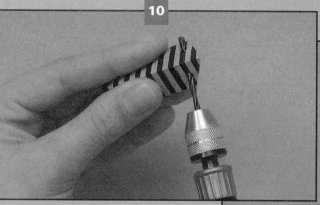

10 Finish off the tigers by drilling a hole for the eyes through the top, close to the pointed end, as shown. Use the mini drill and the ⁷/₆₄-inch bit.

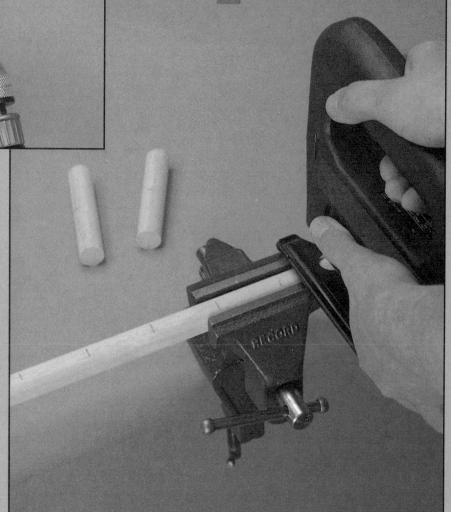

11 Now start making the goat pieces. On the dowel rod, make a series of pencil marks at 45mm (1⁷/₈in) intervals. With the jigsaw and metal cutting blade, cut the rod straight across at the second mark and every alternate mark thereafter. You should have 10 pieces, each with a pencil mark at the centre.

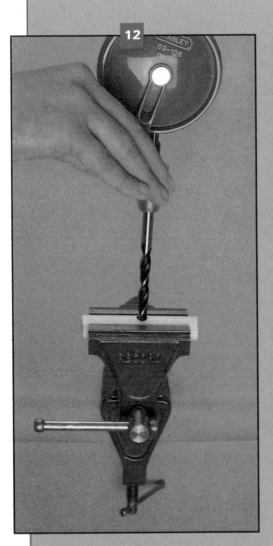

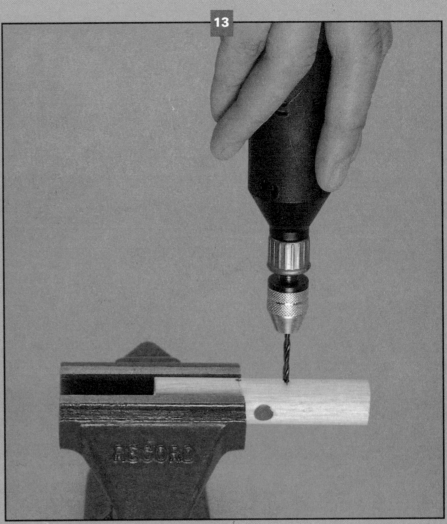

12 Clamp a piece of dowel in the vice and, using the hand drill and the 5/16-inch wood bit, drill a hole right through the rod at the centre mark.

13 Turn the dowel through 90° and, with the mini drill and the 7/64-inch bit, drill two holes right through the middle of the dowel for the eyes, 5mm (3/16in) either side of the large hole. Repeat steps 12 & 13 for each of the goat pieces.

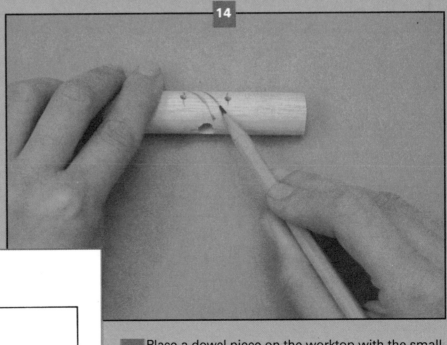

diagram 2

14 Place a dowel piece on the worktop with the small holes facing upwards. Draw a diagonal line across the dowel so that one end is opposite a small hole and the other is at the top of the large hole. Draw a second line parallel to this, relating in the same way to the other small hole (see diagram **2**).

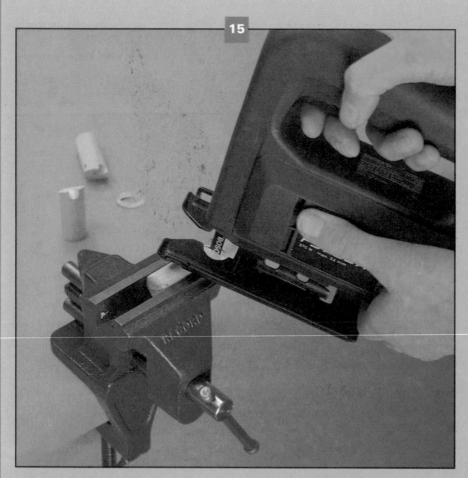

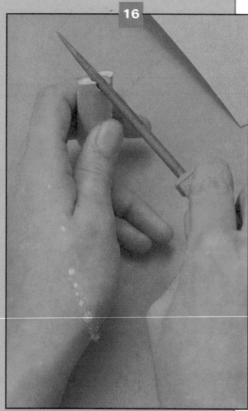

15 Place the piece in the vice and cut along the lines with the jigsaw. By cutting through the centre of the large hole you make the goat's 'horns'.

16 Repeat this process for the rest of the goats (you will now have 20 goats). Finish them off by filing the horns smooth using the 1/4-inch round file.

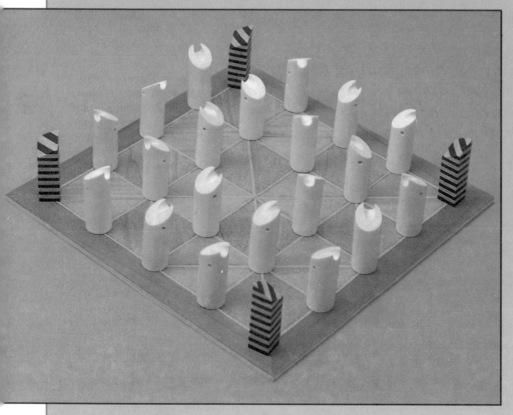

17 Fill the plastic bag with water to check that it doesn't leak. Empty it, then place all the goat pieces in the bag and, following the manufacturer's instructions, use the wood bleach to bleach all the colour from the wood. This may take two applications. Leave the pieces to dry.

You can now reap the reward of all your hard work and relax with family and friends over an absorbing game of 'Goats and tigers'.

SCULPTURE AND 3-D

MOVING SCULPTURE

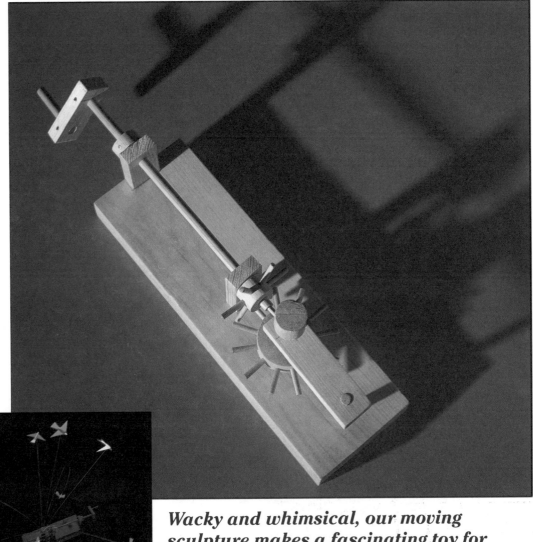

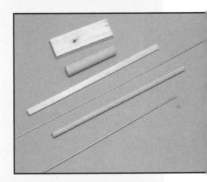

MATERIALS

To make the mechanism for the sculpture shown *below left* you will need:

Above, **3 x 1in timber, 215mm (8¹/₂in) long; ³/₈ x 1in edging strip 200mm (8in) long; ¹/₈in dowel, at least 1m (1yd) long; ¹/₄in dowel, at least 350mm (14in) long; ³/₄in dowel, at least 100mm (4in) long; 15mm (⁵/₈in) length of 1³/₈in dowel; 15mm (⁵/₈in) panel pins; 25mm (1in) panel pin.**

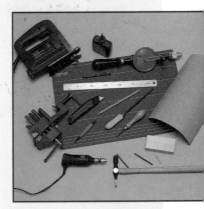

Above, **jigsaw or coping saw; drill (power or hand-held); vice; mini drill; drill bits, sizes 6mm, 3.5mm, 3mm, and 1.3mm (¹/₄in, ⁹/₆₄in, ¹/₈in, ³/₆₄in); round file; small hammer; nail punch; bradawl; craft knife; cutting mat; sandpaper, grade 100; sanding block; wood glue; pencil; metal ruler.**

Wacky and whimsical, our moving sculpture makes a fascinating toy for children and adults alike. When the handle is turned the birds and insects on their wires appear to 'fly'. In the first of a two-part project we show you how to make the movement mechanism.

Our flying bird-and-insect sculpture is called a 'kinetic' sculpture, because the parts move. Kinetic sculptures rely on mechanical power, magnetism or air currents to set them in motion. Mechanically-powered sculpture emerged during the early 1920s, when the Russian sculptor Naum Gabo (1890-1977) made a sculpture consisting of a single oscillating metal rod powered by a hidden electric motor. Later the American sculptor Alexander Calder (1898-1976) exhibited his delicate 'mobiles' (a term he invented) during the 1930s. These consisted of simple counterbalanced weights suspended from wire rods, and relied solely on air currents to create an ever-changing pattern.

Our sculpture has a delicate, light-hearted feel reminiscent of Alexander Calder's mobiles. Tiny wooden birds and insects are threaded on to long, flexible wires mounted on a cog mechanism. When the handle is turned the birds and insects 'fly' round on their wires.

In this first part of the project we show you how to make the cog mechanism — which is a fascinating piece of sculptural engineering in itself. All the pieces are cut from standard timber and dowelling, and then glued or pinned together. It is necessary to be reasonably accurate when constructing the mechanism in order to make it work; however, if it moves a little jerkily this is all part of its charm.

> *HELPFUL HINT*
>
> **Keep any offcuts of wood left over, as you may need them for the second part of this project.**

ASSEMBLY DIAGRAM

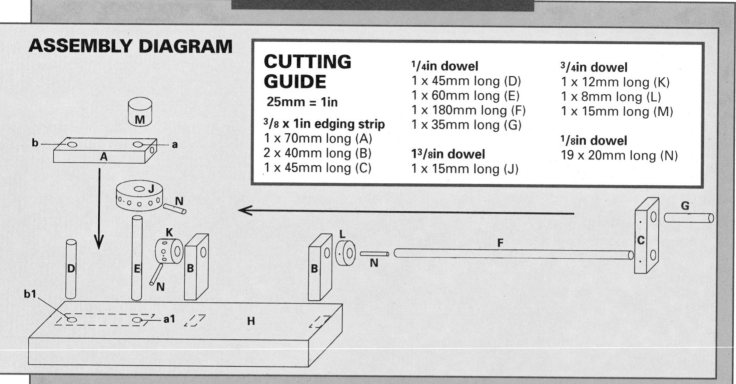

CUTTING GUIDE

25mm = 1in

³/₈ x 1in edging strip
1 x 70mm long (A)
2 x 40mm long (B)
1 x 45mm long (C)

¹/₄in dowel
1 x 45mm long (D)
1 x 60mm long (E)
1 x 180mm long (F)
1 x 35mm long (G)

1³/₈in dowel
1 x 15mm long (J)

³/₄in dowel
1 x 12mm long (K)
1 x 8mm long (L)
1 x 15mm long (M)

¹/₈in dowel
19 x 20mm long (N)

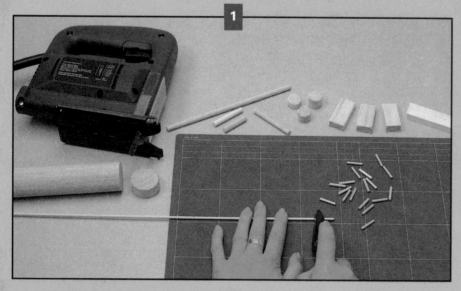

1 Using the jigsaw or craft knife, as appropriate, measure and cut all the pieces needed to make the mechanism, using the cutting guide *above* as reference.

2 To make the main cogwheel, take piece J and measure the length of the circumference by wrapping a strip of paper round it. Lay the paper strip flat and make 12 equally spaced pencil marks along one edge. Wrap it around piece J again and transfer the marks to the wood.

HELPFUL HINT

When drilling holes to a specific depth, mark off the required measurement on the drill bit using a piece of masking tape so that when you are drilling you can see when you have reached the correct depth.

3 Draw a pencil line around the middle of the circumference of piece J. At each of the pencil marks make a hole with the bradawl, exactly on the pencil line. Place the piece in the vice and, using the mini drill and 3mm (¹/₈in) bit, make a hole 5mm (³/₁₆in) deep at each mark, holding the drill vertically.

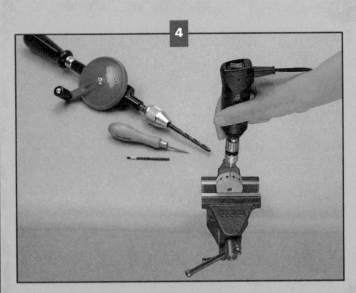

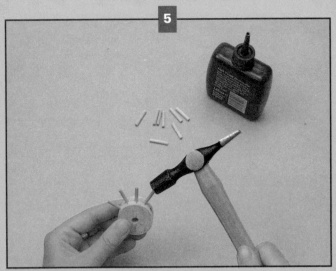

4 Remove the cogwheel from the vice. Lay on its side and mark the centre of the wheel. Starting with the bradawl, use a hand or electric drill to make a 6mm (1/4in) hole right through the centre. Replace the piece in the vice and, with the mini drill and 1.3mm (3/64in) bit, drill a hole between two of the existing holes on the circumference into the centre hole (the wheel will be pinned to its axle through this hole). Sand the wheel.

5 Squeeze a little wood glue into each of the holes around the side of the wheel and insert the spokes (pieces N) into them, tapping them firmly home with the hammer. When the glue is dry, trim the spokes to 15mm (5/8in) with a craft knife.

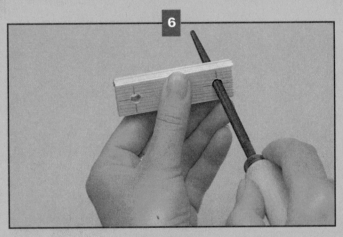

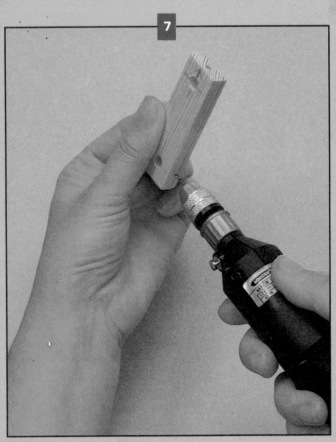

6 Take piece A and drill 6mm (1/4in) holes right through the wood, 10mm (3/8in) in from each end and centred on the width. Using the round file, file out one of the holes to enable the axle (piece E) to turn easily in it. This will be hole a. Leave the other hole (hole b) unfiled to give a tighter fit for support rod D.

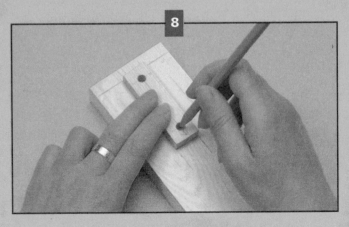

7 With the mini drill and 3.5mm (9/64in) bit, drill a hole 5mm (3/16in) deep into the centre of the end of piece A nearest to hole a. Then drill a 1.3mm (3/64in) hole from the side of piece A into hole b.

8 Lay piece A on the base board, centred on the width and with the end with hole b 10mm (3/8in) from the edge of the base. Draw round piece A to mark its position, then draw through both holes to mark their positions also. Call these holes a1 and b1.

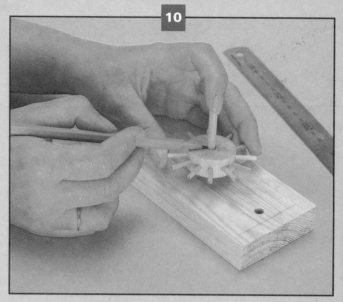

9 With the 6mm (1/4in) bit, drill hole a1 to a depth of 5mm (3/16in). Work the drill around the edge of the hole to enlarge it slightly. Drill hole b1 to a depth of 10mm (3/8in) but do not enlarge it.

10 Push the axle (piece E) into hole a1. Thread the cogwheel on to it so that it clears the base by 5mm (3/16in) and mark its position on the axle.

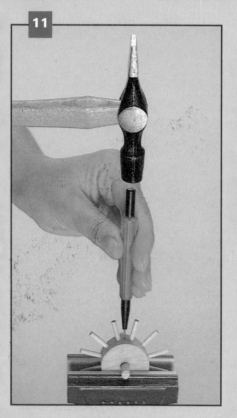

12 Take piece K and, following steps 2-5, make a smaller cogwheel with six spokes. Drill a 6mm (1/4in) hole right through the centre of piece L, then drill a 1.3mm (3/64in) hole from the side through to the centre hole.

13 Drill a 6mm (1/4in) hole 10mm (3/8in) in from one end (centred on the width) of both pieces B. File out the holes to allow the axle F to turn easily. Drill 6mm (1/4in) holes 10mm (3/8in) in from each end of piece C (centred on the width). Drill 1.3mm (3/64in) pinning holes from the sides into the 6mm (1/4in) holes.

11 Keeping the cogwheel in position on the axle, remove it from the hole and place in the vice. Using the hammer and nail punch, drive a 25mm (1in) panel pin through the hole in the cogwheel into the axle to fix in place.

14 In one end of the axle F, carefully drill a 3mm (1/8in) hole 5mm (3/16in) deep. Glue the remaining piece N into this hole and tap home with the hammer.

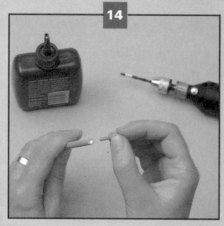

15

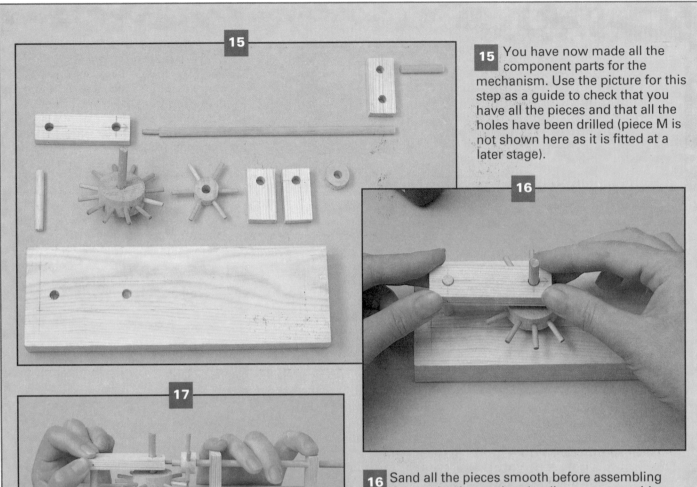

15 You have now made all the component parts for the mechanism. Use the picture for this step as a guide to check that you have all the pieces and that all the holes have been drilled (piece M is not shown here as it is fitted at a later stage).

16

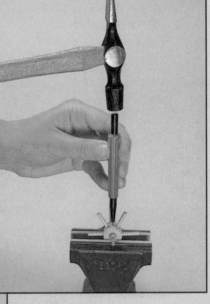

16 Sand all the pieces smooth before assembling the mechanism, using the diagram as a guide. Push the axle E of the large cogwheel into hole a1 and the support rod D into hole b1. Glue support rod D in place. Fit piece A on to the axle E and support rod D but do not fix it in place yet.

17

17 Thread the two pieces B on to axle F, then thread the smaller cogwheel on to one end of the axle. Position the pieces roughly as shown, but do not fix in place. Push piece N on axle F into the hole on piece A. Supporting the pieces on axle F with one hand, adjust the height of the piece A on its support rod D so that it is level with axle F; mark its position and fix it with a 15mm (5/8in) panel pin.

18

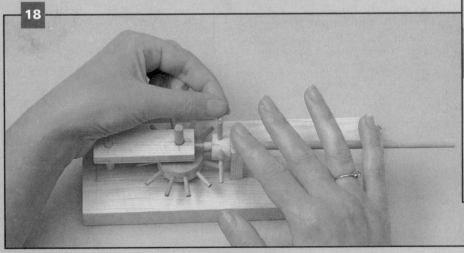

Mark the position of the small wheel on the axle, then remove them, still together, and place in the vice. Using a hammer and nail punch, fix the wheel to the axle with a 15mm (5/8in) panel pin (see inset).

18 The spokes on the small wheel must connect with the spokes on the large wheel in order to drive the large wheel when the handle is turned; move the small wheel along the axle until the spokes engage.

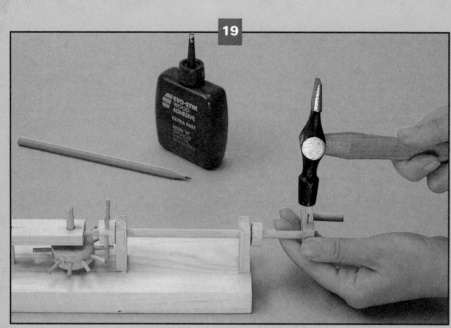

19 Thread the two axle supports B on to axle F again and re-connect it to piece A. Position one axle support at the edge of the base board and push the other tight against the small wheel. Mark their positions on the base board with pencil, then glue them in place (you can nail, screw or peg them from the bottom of the base if you prefer). Push the washer L on to the axle and up against the end rod support. Pin it to the axle. To make the handle, push piece C on to the end of the axle, then push piece G into the remaining hole in piece C. Fix with 15mm (5/8in) panel pins.

20 Trim support rod D at hole b flush with the top of piece A. Turn the handle to test that the mechanism works smoothly; if the cogwheels are sticking, trim a little from their spokes. Drill a 7mm (1/4in)-deep hole into the centre of piece M using the 6mm (1/4in) bit. Put some glue in the hole and glue it to the top of the large cogwheel axle E. This forms the base for the bird wires, which you will place in position in part two of this project.

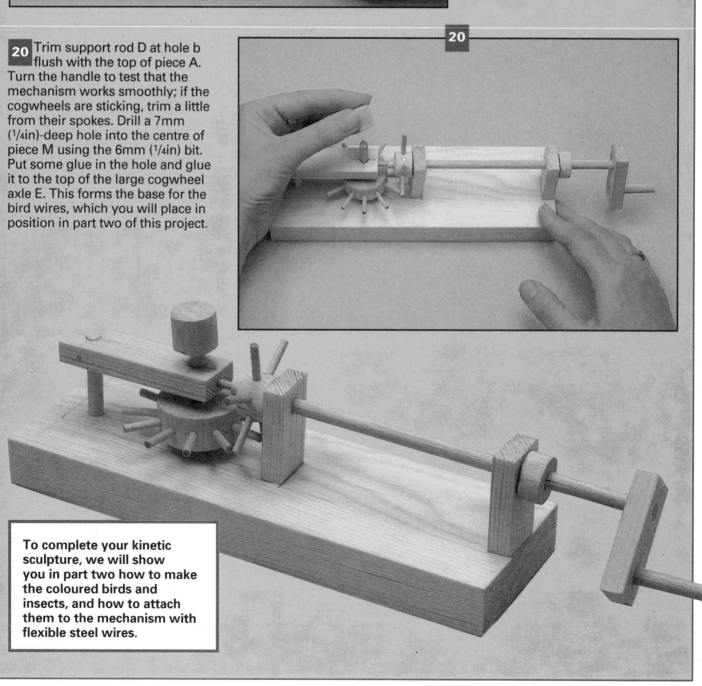

To complete your kinetic sculpture, we will show you in part two how to make the coloured birds and insects, and how to attach them to the mechanism with flexible steel wires.

SCULPTURE AND 3-D

MOVING SCULPTURE

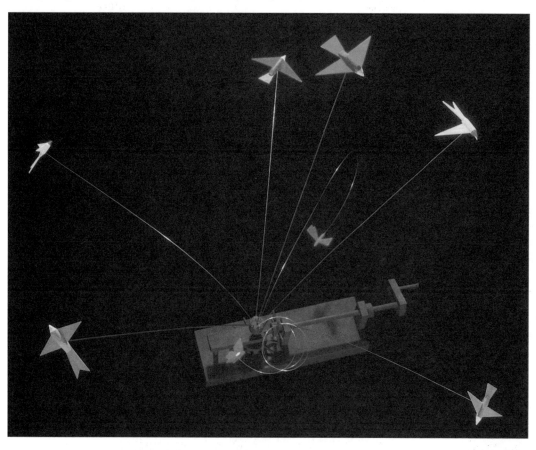

MATERIALS

To complete the moving sculpture shown *below left* you will need:

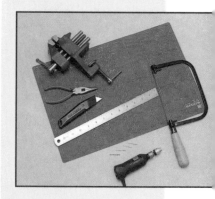

Above, vice; coping saw; mini drill; drill bits, 0.5mm, 0.8mm and 1.3mm (1/64in, 1/32in and 3/64in); craft knife; metal ruler; cutting mat; pliers with wirecutters.

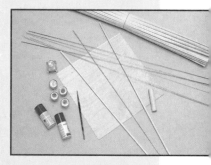

Above, sheet of 1/32in plywood, 300 x 300mm (12 x 12in); short lengths of 1/8in, 1/4in, 3/4in and 5/16in dowel (you can use any offcuts left over from making the mechanism); 1m (1yd) lengths of steel wire, 0.015in, 0.025in, 0.032in, 0.047in, 0.055in; 2 x 1m (1yd) lengths of 0.020in steel wire; small cans of spray paint, matt white and matt black; small tins of enamel paint, fluorescent orange, pink, yellow and green; small bottle of cellulose thinner; small paintbrush; sheets of newsprint.
You will also need sandpaper and wood glue.

In part two of our moving sculpture project we make the brightly coloured birds and insects that 'fly' on long flexible wires, and show you how to connect them to the cog mechanism that makes them move.

Having done the serious work of making the cog mechanism, you are now ready for the 'fun' part — making the sculpture itself. The six birds and two insects are mounted on long 'stalks' of flexible steel wire, which seems to give them a life of their own; not only do they rotate as the handle is turned, but they also bounce and wave in the air.

Flying high
The creatures are made of thin plywood, which means that they are light enough to be supported by the wires, but heavy enough to bounce when lightly touched with the finger. In keeping with the eccentric mood of the piece, we have painted the creatures in fluorescent colours; because the colours are so bright, they seem

to come forward, and this has the effect of making the birds and insects seem quite independent from the base of the model, which is painted matt black. Placing the sculpture in a dark room, under an ultra-violet light, would create an even more dramatic effect, as the creatures would appear to be flying independently of their wires.

113

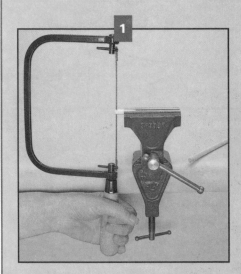

1 To make the body of the first bird, cut a 30mm (1³/₁₆in) length of ¹/₄in dowel and place it in the vice as shown. Using the coping saw, carefully make a slit 5mm (³/₁₆in) long in one end of the dowel. This is the slot for the tail.

2 Inserting the teeth of the blade into the slit just made, saw a lengthwise slit, about 2mm (¹/₁₆in) deep, along the length of the dowel. Turn the dowel over and make another slit on the opposite side to the same depth. These slots are for the wings.

3 Remove the piece from the vice. Starting 5mm (³/₁₆in) or so back from the tail slit, use a sharp craft knife to whittle away some of the wood so that the upper body tapers towards the tail slit. Turn over and repeat for the underside.

4 Starting 5mm (³/₁₆in) or so from the front of the body, shape the bird's head by whittling the wood to a point all the way round, as though you were sharpening a pencil.

5 On the sheet of plywood draw the shapes of the wings and the tail (see diagram **1**). Cut them out using a sharp craft knife held against a metal ruler.

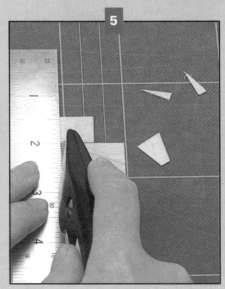

diagram 1

bird tail

bird wings

direction of grain

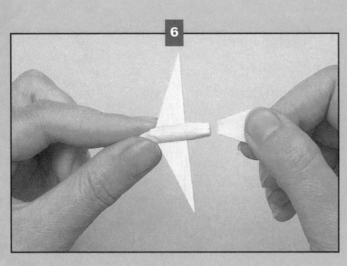

diagram 2

direction of grain

alternative wing and tail shapes

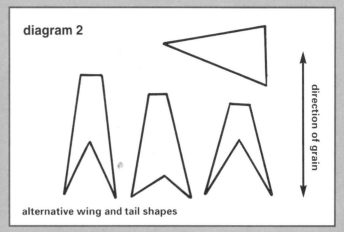

6 Smooth off the slots with a piece of sandpaper folded in two. Squeeze a tiny drop of wood glue along the short edge of a wing piece and push it into one of the wing slots. Do the same with the other wing and the tail.

7 Make three more birds in the same way using the ¹/₄in dowel, and another two with the ⁵/₁₆in dowel. To give added interest, vary the angles of the wings, and the shapes of the wings and tails, using diagram **2** as a guide.

8 To make the dragonfly, cut a 25mm (1in) length of ¹/₈in dowel and sharpen both ends to a 'pencil point' with the craft knife.

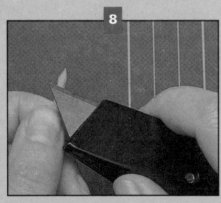

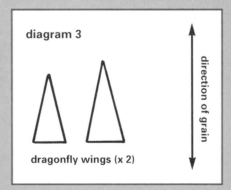

diagram 3

direction of grain

dragonfly wings (x 2)

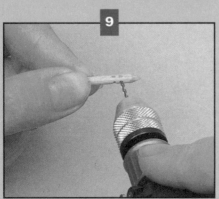

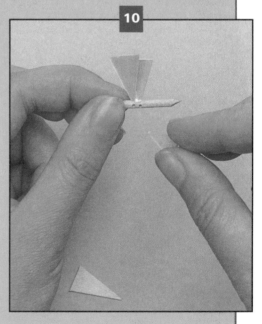

9 Using the 1.3mm (³/₆₄in) bit, drill two tiny holes on either side of the body, starting 1cm (³/₈in) from one end. Drill at an angle of 30° to the horizontal, 1.5mm (¹/₁₆in) deep and 3mm (¹/₈in) apart.

10 Cut out two each of the small and large dragonfly wings (see diagram **3**) on the sheet of plywood, trimming a tiny piece from the sharp point of each one.

Glue the wings into the holes in the body, pointing upwards as shown, the larger pair at the front. Leave the dragonfly carefully propped up until the glue has dried.

11 To make the butterfly, cut out the two wing shapes (see diagram **4**) and slot them together at right angles.

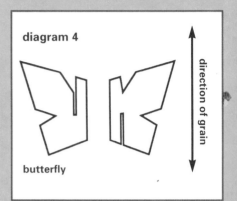

diagram 4

direction of grain

butterfly

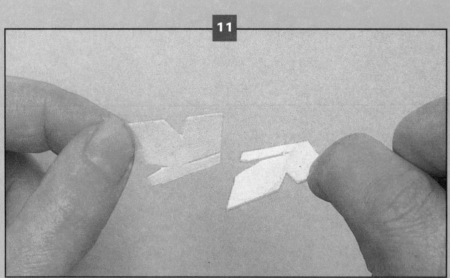

11

12

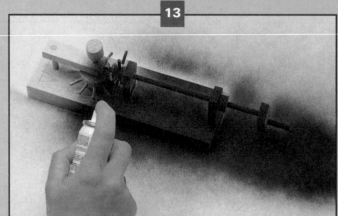

13

12 Lay out all the creatures on a sheet of newsprint and spray them with white spray paint. Leave until touch-dry, then give them another coat, ensuring that they are completely covered.

13 While the birds and insects are drying, take the cog mechanism outdoors and spray it with black spray paint. Spray it lightly from several angles to get at all the surfaces, then leave to dry. Turn the cogs to get at the parts that are hidden, and spray again.

14 The birds are painted with different combinations of colours, but to the same pattern: paint the back, wings and tail one colour, the breast patch another, and the beak either orange or yellow. Mix the enamel paints with just a little cellulose thinner and apply the paint with a small paintbrush.

14

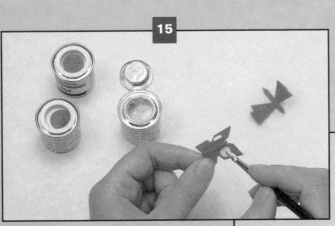

15 Paint the butterfly one colour all over. Leave to dry, then paint a round dot in a contrasting colour on each wing. Paint the dragonfly, using one colour on the body and another on the wings.

16 Choose one of the larger birds. Using the 0.8mm ($^{1}/_{32}$in) drill bit, drill a hole in the underside of the bird, a little further than halfway through its body.

17 With the wirecutters, cut a 55cm (22in) length of 0.055in steel wire (bend it with the pliers to snap it off). Push one end of the wire into the hole in the underside of the bird (if it is a little loose put a drop of wood glue on the end of the wire). Drill a 0.8mm ($^{1}/_{32}$in) hole 10mm ($^{3}/_{8}$in) deep in the centre of the rotating head (piece M) on the base mechanism. Push the other end of the wire into the hole.

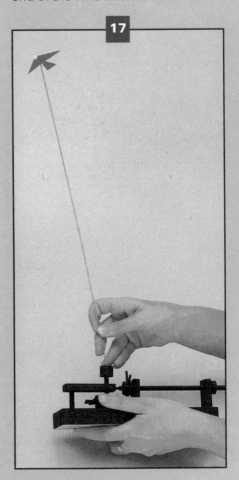

18 Fix the remaining birds in the same way, using different thicknesses of steel wire depending on the size and weight of the bird; use 0.020 or 0.025 wire for the smallest birds, and 0.032 or 0.047 wire for the bigger ones. Vary the lengths of the wires between approximately 34cm (13in) and 46cm (18in). Drill holes in the rotating head at a slight angle, evenly spaced around the central one, and push the ends of the wires firmly home.

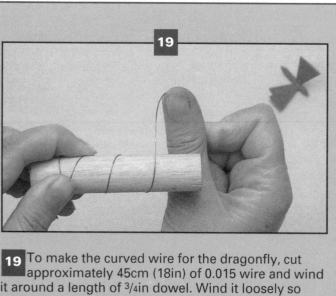

19 To make the curved wire for the dragonfly, cut approximately 45cm (18in) of 0.015 wire and wind it around a length of ³/₄in dowel. Wind it loosely so that when you let it go it makes a gently arching curve.

20 Drill two 0.8mm (¹/₃₂in) holes, 3mm (¹/₈in) apart, through the dragonfly's body, just behind the wings. Thread one end of the wire through the body,

bend it along to the next hole and thread it back up. Drill a vertical hole in the rotating head, between any two wires, and plant the other end of the wire into it.

HELPFUL HINT

Experiment with the butterfly spring to see how it works best — you may need to tighten or loosen the coil, or pass it behind the adjacent wires to steady it and hold it in the right position.

21 Make the coiled spring for the butterfly in the same way as in step 19, but use a length of 0.020 wire about 80cm (30in) long and wind it much more tightly around the dowel. Thread the wire through the butterfly's body as in step 20. Drill a vertical hole in the rotating head, opposite where you placed the dragonfly, and push the end of the wire home.

Turn the handle of the cog mechanism and see your birds and insects fly around in a most beguiling manner. Placed under dramatic lighting, your kinetic sculpture will have even more impact.

PRINTMAKING

PRINTMAKING

DECORATIVE WOODCUT

MATERIALS

To print the stationery as shown *below left* you need:

Above, block of softwood, 85 x 43mm (3¹/₂ x 1³/₄in) and approx. 17mm (⁵/₈in) thick; 4 pieces of wood of the thickness of the woodblock — two pieces 100 x 370mm (4 x 14¹/₂in), one piece 87 x 125mm (3¹/₂ x 5in) and one piece 87 x 200mm (3¹/₂ x 8in); pencil; tracing paper; carbon paper; masking tape.

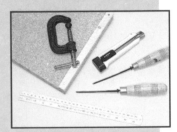

Above, craft knife; woodcutter's V-shaped gouge; flat U-shaped chisel; jig; G-clamp; steel ruler.

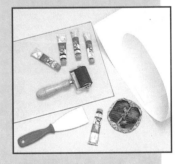

Above, one to five tubes of oil-based printing inks in colours of your choice; paint scraper or palette knife; paper to cut into approximately 20 A4 (11⁵/₈ x 8¹/₄in) sheets , for printing; sheet of glass, approximately 280 x 200mm (11 x 8in); baren; 25mm (1in) rubber roller.

This project gives you the opportunity to develop your skills in making relief prints, and also introduces you to some of the basic techniques of woodcarving. We have used these techniques to produce a small woodblock, which can be used to great effect for handprinting your stationery.

Carving a design into the surface of a small wooden block and then inking the block and taking a woodprint is one of the many means of transferring an image from one surface to another. The simplicity and starkness of the resulting relief prints give them a special charm of their own.

The use of wood for printmaking is particularly interesting, because it offers endless possibilities for variety and invention, and at the same time demands very little experience or expense. The images you make can be simple or complex, bold and colourful or elegant and subtle, and can be used for a variety of purposes — for instance, you could create a woodcut incorporating your name or initials to personalise your books.

You can use any type and colour of paper to print your stationery, providing that it is neither too textured nor too thick. Stiff paper is unsuitable for handprinting as it requires more pressure on the block than can be achieved with a baren. Oil-based printing inks give the best results, and are available in a wide variety of colours. They are also easy to mix, so if you cannot find the precise colour you can always make your own. When you have finished printing, the ink can be easily removed from materials with white spirit.

HELPFUL HINT

Some printing inks need a little linseed oil mixed with them to give the ink the creamy consistency that is necessary for printing. Ask your supplier for advice when purchasing your inks.

THE TEMPLATE

The shaded parts of the template are the areas of the design that will not be printed — that is, those areas that you must cut away from your block. When you have traced the template (see Step 1) it is a good idea to copy the shaded areas on to your tracing and keep this beside you as a guide when you are cutting your block, so that you do not cut into the areas that will be printed.

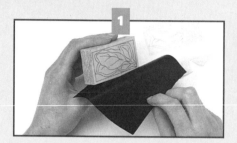

1 Trace the template on to a piece of tracing paper. Decide which way you want to print the

block (that is, with the leaf stalk on the righthand or lefthand side) and reverse the tracing, so that when you print the block on your stationery the design will appear the right way round. Put a piece of carbon paper (carbon side down) between the tracing and the wood block and attach them to the wood block with masking tape. Go over the design with a pencil. Remove the tracing and carbon paper.

HELPFUL HINT

Remember to keep the hand that is supporting the woodblock well out of the way when you are cutting. Always place the block up against the edge of the jig and make certain that the block is well secured by the G-clamp.

2 Use the G-clamp to secure the wood to the jig and the work surface. Place a pad of folded paper between the block and the clamp, as shown, to avoid bruising the surface of the wood. Use the V-shaped gouge to cut away the thin lines of the border. (You will have to turn your block to cut the border at the other end.)

3 Use the U-shaped chisel to clear away the large areas. To make cutting easier, use a craft knife to outline the perimeter of the

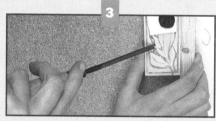

large areas before you use the chisel (see Using the craft knife). This will prevent the wood splintering when you reach the edges of these shapes with your U-chisel.

USING THE CRAFT KNIFE

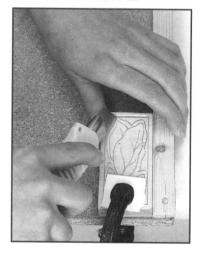

When outlining the perimeter of large areas with a craft knife, hold the knife at an angle. As you cut along the outside line, angle the knife towards you, as shown. As you cut along the inside line, angle the knife away from you, so that you get a V-shaped channel. Once you have outlined the whole area, use the V-shaped gouge to cut away the areas between the two knife-cut lines.

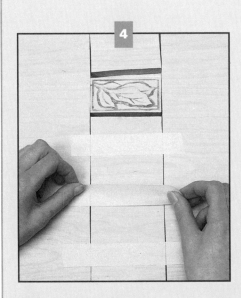

4 Place your woodblock on your work surface and surround it with your extra pieces of wood to make the printing base, as shown. Put masking tape across the printing base to hold the pieces of wood in place.

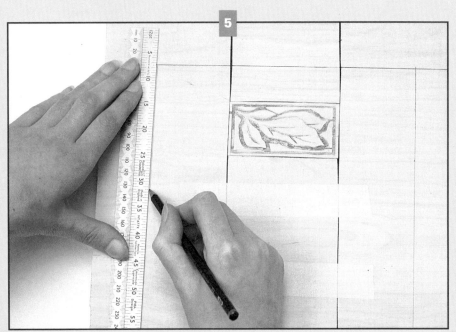

5 To make certain you place your paper in the correct position when printing, simply draw a line 15mm ($^5/_8$in) from the top of the printing base and 38.5mm ($1^1/_2$in) from each side, as shown.

6 Squeeze some printing ink on to a sheet of glass. Use it straight from the tube or mix it with a little white or black to lighten or darken the colour. The ink should have a creamy consistency; if it is too thick, add a little linseed oil to it, but use it sparingly. Mix thoroughly with your mixing knife.

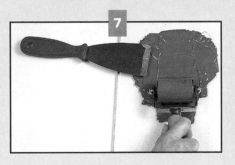

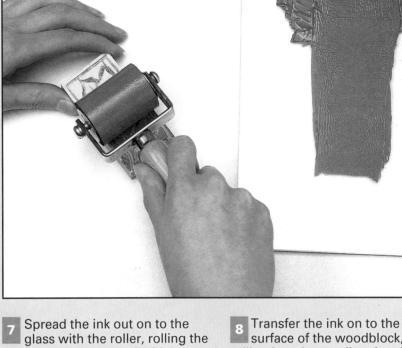

7 Spread the ink out on to the glass with the roller, rolling the ink in one direction only. Make sure you have an even skin of ink over the whole surface of the roller.

8 Transfer the ink on to the surface of the woodblock, again rolling in only one direction. Re-ink the roller and repeat if necessary.

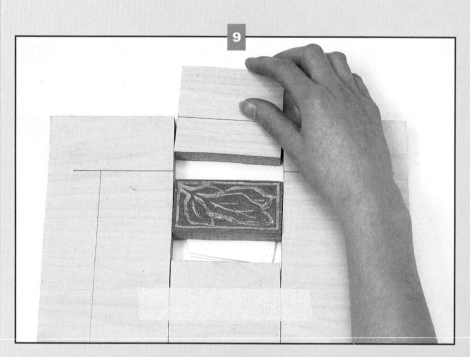

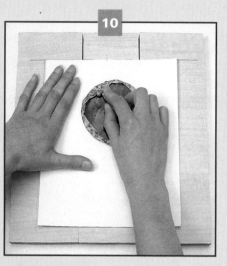

9 Place the woodblock in the printing base, putting a small piece of folded paper under the woodblock first, as shown, so that the block is slightly raised above the printing base.

10 Place your printing paper over the inked woodblock, aligning it with your pencilled guidelines. Burnish the back of the paper with the baren, using a circular motion. You may have to make a few test prints before the ink 'settles' into the woodblock.

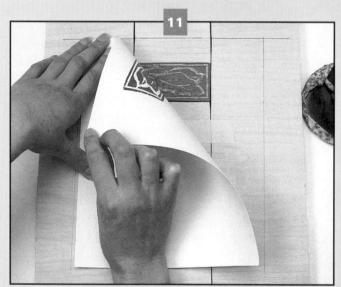

SHARPENING YOUR TOOLS

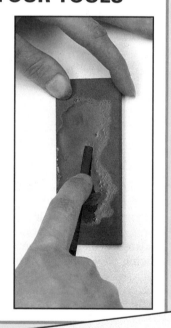

You will get the best results when cutting a woodblock by keeping your tools sharp. To sharpen them, put a drop of 3-in-1 oil on an oilstone (available from suppliers of woodcutting tools). Rub the gouge or chisel over the surface of the stone, starting at the top and making a figure-of-eight. As you move the tool over the surface of the stone turn it from side to side. Continue until the tool is sufficiently sharp.

11 Carefully peel your print off the block, pulling diagonally from one corner to the other. Lay your printed paper in a safe place to dry (it will take about 24 hours for the ink to dry thoroughly). Continue printing, re-inking your block as necessary, until you have completed all your prints.

You can use your woodblock to decorate envelopes to match your letterheads, and also to personalise plain postcards or business cards. Another idea is to print your own gift wrap, either printing at random on the surface of the paper or aligning the prints in regular rows over the surface.

SCULPTURE AND 3-D

FISH WOODCARVING

MATERIALS

To make the woodcarving shown *below left* you will need:

Above, carbon paper; ruler; sketch paper; scissors; pencil; hardwood, 240 x 152 x 25mm (9^{1}/$_{2}$ x 6 x 1in).

Above, masking tape; parting tool (V-shaped gouge), ^{3}/$_{16}$in (no 39); two curved gouges, ^{1}/$_{4}$in (no 5), ^{1}/$_{2}$in (no 8); two riffler files, square and round profile; wood mallet; sandpaper, medium and fine grade; large G-clamp; beeswax furniture cream; soft cloth.

We introduced you to the basic techniques of relief woodcarving in the decorative woodcut project. Now we develop these techniques and put them to use on a larger scale to produce a decorative fish carved in relief.

Carving is the most traditional method of making a sculpture. It is an extremely rewarding and direct way of re-shaping a material into a new form and has existed ever since man was capable of producing tools sharp enough to make an impression on another material.

The carving process is entirely subtractive — once you have carved away an area of wood there is no opportunity for replacing it, as you might if you were modelling with clay, for example. The knowledge that each change you make is critical and unalterable adds to the excitement and the need for precision in carving. The relief carving of the fish will create a shallow three-dimensional form, carved to two different depths, so creating a design with three distinct layers.

Tool care
We recommend that you start with three gouges. You may need to sharpen them before you use them (some suppliers only sell unsharpened tools) and it is important

to have them re-sharpened from time to time. Instructions for sharpening your own tools are given in the next project (see toucan carving). Alternatively, you could have them sharpened professionally. Mallets are available in different weights, and you should choose one that you feel comfortable with, and that is suitable for the project you are working on. Once you have covered the initial expense of the tools they will, with care, last a lifetime. You will soon become familiar with the range of cuts that each tool will make.

The right wood
Your selection of wood is important and provides plenty of opportunity for experimenting. However, for your first carving it is advisable to choose a fine-grained hardwood. This lends itself to reasonably easy carving and is unlikely to splinter when you are carving across the grain. We have used limewood for this project, but cherry or magnolia would be equally suitable.

HELPFUL HINT

To design you own woodcarving panel, first make a number of simple pencil sketches on paper, working to the correct size. You will see the various features of a carving begin to take shape through these sketches, and the sketch lines define both form and detail. When you are happy with the basic outlines, add the detail.

When you have a final design, transfer the outlines of the sketch onto the block of wood, either directly in pencil or using the method explained in step 1 overleaf.

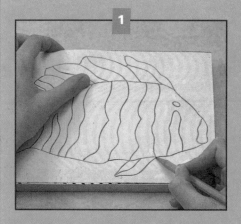

1 Photocopy the template at 200%. Cut out the template (around the rectangular edge) and cut a piece of carbon paper to the same size. If necessary, smooth the top surface of the wood block with sandpaper. Tape the carbon paper and the template to the wood and go over the outline with a pencil to transfer the design.

THE TEMPLATE

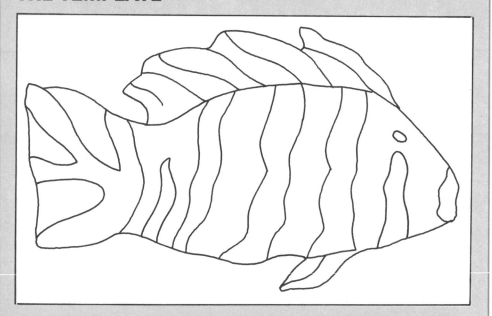

2 Secure the wood to the table with a G-clamp, placing a small pad of paper between the wood and the clamp to protect the wood. Place the point of the parting tool on the outline of the fish, and, holding the gouge at an angle of about 40° to the wood, tap gently with the mallet to carve a channel around the silhouette of the fish. Keep the gouge at the same angle as you work along the channel, and do not dig down too deeply. Re-position the wood in the clamp as necessary to work around the shape.

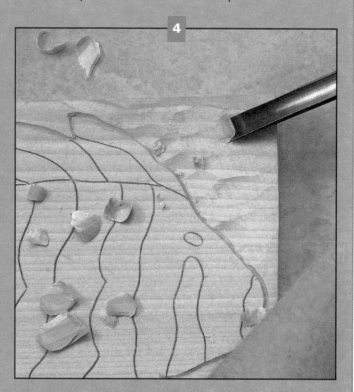

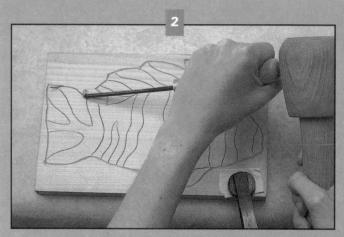

3 Use the large curved gouge to carve away the wood immediately outside the silhouette of the fish, working towards the channel, and taking care not to go deeper than this line.

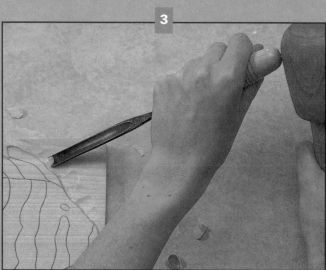

4 Continue to carve away the wood outside the outline of the fish to the same depth.

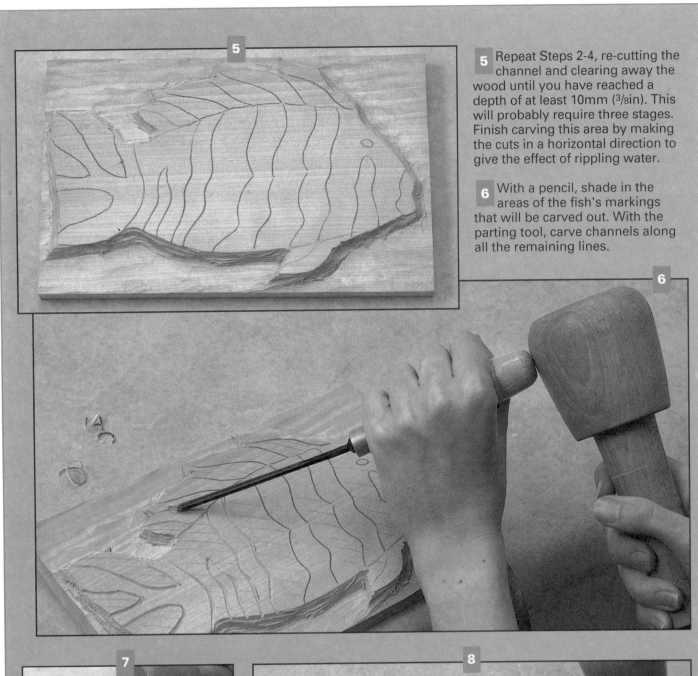

5 Repeat Steps 2-4, re-cutting the channel and clearing away the wood until you have reached a depth of at least 10mm ($^3/_8$in). This will probably require three stages. Finish carving this area by making the cuts in a horizontal direction to give the effect of rippling water.

6 With a pencil, shade in the areas of the fish's markings that will be carved out. With the parting tool, carve channels along all the remaining lines.

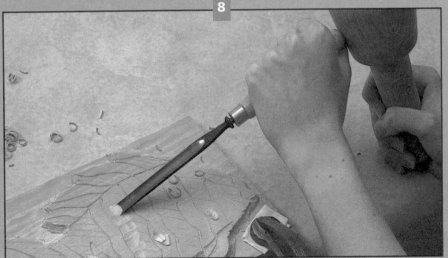

7 Hold the small curved gouge vertically, and tap with the mallet to make three or four cuts around the eye.

8 Carve away the areas in the body, tail and fins, starting with the large gouge, working first on one side of the shape, then re-positioning the wood to carve the other side. Use the small curved gouge for the smaller areas, curves and angles.

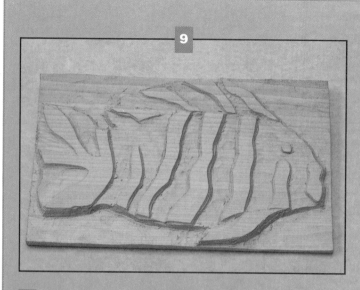

9 Re-cut the channels with the parting tool and clear out the wood with the curved gouges until the carved area reaches a depth of 5mm (3/16in).

10 Smooth the edges of the carving by filing around them with the square riffler. Use the round riffler for tight corners.

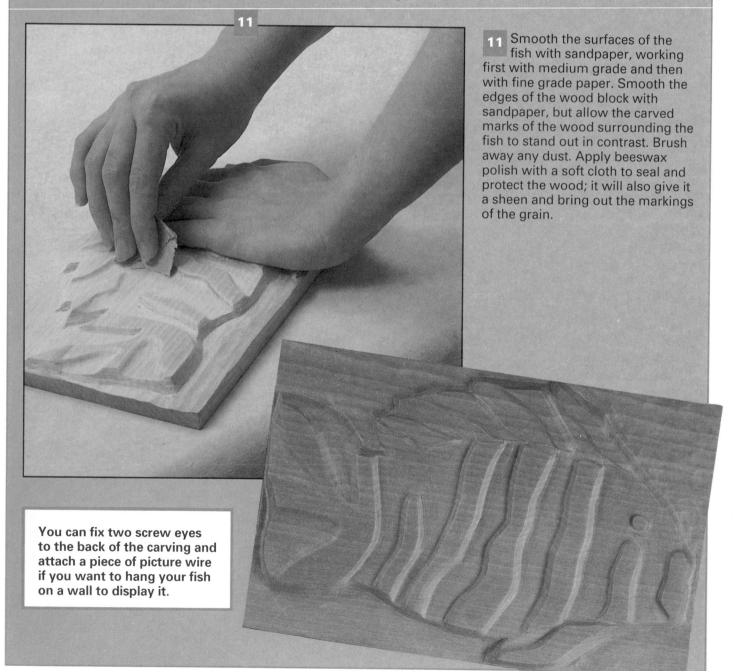

11 Smooth the surfaces of the fish with sandpaper, working first with medium grade and then with fine grade paper. Smooth the edges of the wood block with sandpaper, but allow the carved marks of the wood surrounding the fish to stand out in contrast. Brush away any dust. Apply beeswax polish with a soft cloth to seal and protect the wood; it will also give it a sheen and bring out the markings of the grain.

You can fix two screw eyes to the back of the carving and attach a piece of picture wire if you want to hang your fish on a wall to display it.

SCULPTURE AND 3-D

TOUCAN CARVING

MATERIALS

To make the painted carving shown *below left* you will need:

Above, piece of 20mm (3/4in) parana pine, 395 x 288mm (15¹/2 x 11³/8in) cut to the shape of the template (see next page); small gouge (1/4in); medium gouge (1/2in); small chisel (1/4in); mallet; fine oilstone; slip stone; light lubricating oil; kitchen roll; medium grade sandpaper and small wooden block; newsprint; masking tape; ruler; G-clamp; craft knife; pencils, 2B and H; red pencil.

Above, PVA wood glue; white emulsion; polyurethane gloss varnish; 2 decorator's brushes; watercolour brushes, large, medium and small; 2 jam jars; black water-soluble ink; waterproof drawing inks, blue, viridian, purple, carmine, sunshine yellow, nut brown; black Indian ink.

Following on from our relief fish woodcarving project, we now show you how to achieve the illusion of three-dimensional form and space by carving and painting a colourful toucan panel on a piece of parana pine.

Our carved and painted toucan panel takes its inspiration from the traditional 'folk' relief carvings of Africa, the Americas and the South Pacific, which were fashioned with simple tools and often decorated in primary colours. We have used parana pine, a soft wood, for the project. We have used the same gouges that we used for the relief fish carving, but here we use a smaller chisel. This is used to carve a channel around the outline of the design to keep subsequent carving (with the chisel and gouges) in the right areas. Carving should be worked mainly along the direction of the grain of the wood, using short, shallow strokes. Be ready to stop if the tool begins to cut too deeply. Before painting, the panel is sealed with diluted PVA wood glue. Areas that are to remain as highlights are given a coat of white emulsion, and inks are used to add colour. In the carved areas, the ink settles into the grooves and hollows and adds to the textural interest.

THE TEMPLATE

288mm (11¼in)

SHARPENING YOUR TOOLS

Remember to keep your tools sharp as you work on the project.

Chisels
Dribble a little light oil on the oilstone. Hold the chisel at an angle of about 30º to the horizontal, with the bevelled side of the blade on the stone, and draw it backwards and forwards across the oilstone until the cutting edge is keen and sharp. Remove the bur by drawing the flat edge of the blade across the stone.

Gouges
Apply a few drops of oil to the oilstone. Hold the gouge at a 30º angle and draw it across the stone in a figure-of-eight pattern, simultaneously rocking the gouge with a wrist motion so that the entire surface of the bevel comes into contact with the stone, **1**. Continue until the edge is keen. Remove the bur on the inner bevel with an oiled circular or shaped slip stone, **2**.

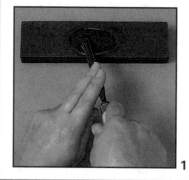

CUTTING THE WOOD

Photocopy the template at 200% and then again at 160% and cut around the edges of the design. Take the design to your local timber merchant and select a piece of parana pine (watch out for imperfections such as knots and blemishes). Have the piece cut and shaped (the grain of the wood should run lengthwise). If they will not shape the wood for you, you can do this yourself using a jigsaw (which can usually be hired by the day), but make sure that you buy a piece of wood longer than the required length to allow for cutting. Alternatively, use a rectangular piece of wood.

1 Wrap a piece of sandpaper around a small block of wood to make a sanding block and smooth the edges of the wood, taking care to achieve a smooth curve at the top.

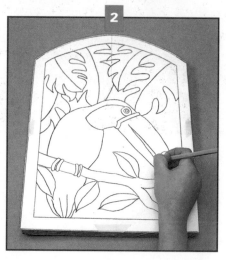

2 Rub over the reverse side of the enlarged template (see Cutting the wood, *left*) with a 2B pencil, then turn it over, secure to the panel with masking tape and go over the outlines with pencil to transfer the design. Remove the template and strengthen the traced lines with a hard pencil.

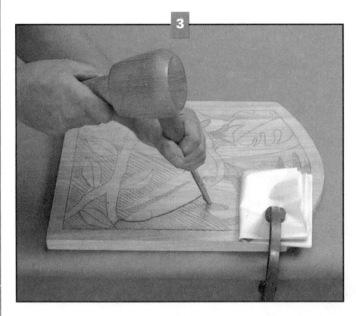

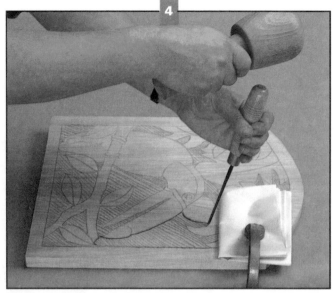

3 On the wood, shade the areas shown in black on the template with a red pencil to indicate the areas that are to be deeply carved. Cover your work table with newsprint and clamp the panel tightly to the surface with a G-clamp, placing a wad of paper between the clamp and the panel to prevent pressure marks. With the mallet and chisel, cut a channel around the outlines of the red areas, making a series of small adjacent cuts. Hold the chisel at a near-vertical angle, with the flat cutting edge facing the line.

4 When cutting around tight curves, use the small gouge as shown to give greater control.

5 Carve out the area shaded in red above the toucan's beak using the chisel and mallet, following the direction of the wood grain (you can carve slightly across the grain, but cutting straight across the grain may cause the wood to split). Hold the chisel at a shallow angle and tap it gently with the mallet. If necessary, re-cut areas of the outline channels (steps 3 and 4) to prevent cutting into the wrong areas, or to deepen the area of the carving if required.

6 Continue chiselling out until you reach the required depth (approximately 5mm/¼in). For an interesting texture, scoop out hollows with the large gouge, again in the direction of the grain.

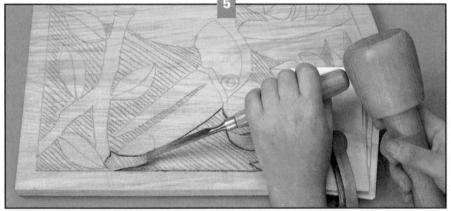

7 Where the toucan's beak narrows, use the chisel without the mallet to simply lift out the sliver of wood between the channels. Continue chiselling out all the areas shaded red, and use the large and small gouges to give a texture to these areas.

8 Use the chisel and mallet to cut channels to cut the remaining lines and the veins of the leaves at the top of the design as in steps 3 and 4. With the large gouge, without the mallet, remove the surface of the two top central leaves and the leaf on the left to give the illusion that they are behind the other two leaves.

9 Using the small gouge, make small marks to represent feathers on the toucan's body and neck, using a light scooping motion. With the small gouge and the mallet, carve veins on the leaves at the base of the design and gouge out linear marks on the branches to represent the rough texture of bark.

10 Use the point of the craft knife to lightly score the remaining outlines (the claws, the lines on the beak and the eye). Do not attempt to 'draw' the circles of the eye with the knife, but use a press-and-lift motion with the point of the blade, working gradually around the lines. Keep your fingers well away from the blade!

11 Brush the wood chips and dust from the panel. Dilute one part PVA wood glue with two parts water and, using a decorator's brush, apply this over the entire surface of the panel, including the edges. This seals the wood and prepares the surface for painting. It also prevents colours from bleeding into each other. Leave to dry for 10 minutes.

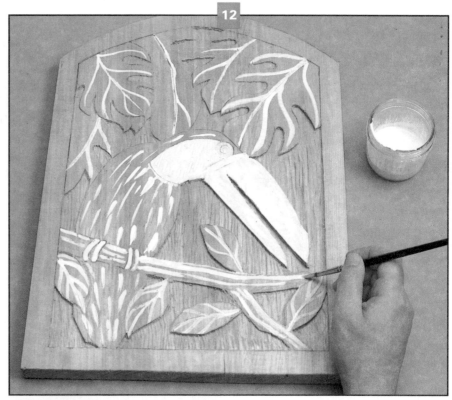

12 Thin some white emulsion paint with a little water. Using a round watercolour brush, paint those parts of the design which are to be lightest in colour as shown. Leave to dry.

13 Using a clean brush, apply a wash of sunshine yellow ink over the areas shown. Note that the colour appears much brighter where it overlays white.

14 Apply a wash of viridian ink over the upper leaves, mixing a little water with the ink in some areas on the panel and pushing the colour around to give a mottled effect. The veins of the leaves, which were underpainted with white, appear much lighter.

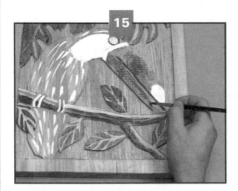

15 Using the nut brown and carmine inks mixed on the wood, paint the lower half of the branch to give an impression of shadow. Paint the areas between the veins of the lower leaves with the same colour. Add a wash of carmine over the yellow of the beak to deepen the colour.

16 To enhance the three-dimensional effect, apply a wash of blue ink diluted with water to darken the two top central leaves and the leaf on the left at the top of the panel. Use undiluted blue ink to paint the toucan's feathers. When this is dry, add darker feathers with black water-soluble ink.

17 Use black Indian ink to paint the bird's eye and the base and tip of the beak. Finally, paint the background with purple ink, adding water to the colour in some areas and washes of blue in other areas to give variety to the colour. Leave to dry overnight. With a decorator's brush, apply a coat of gloss varnish over the entire panel.

If you want to retain some of the natural wood, leave the background unpainted. To display your carving on the wall, fix two screw eyes to the back and attach a length of picture wire.

SCULPTURE AND 3-D

SALAD SERVERS

MATERIALS

To make the salad servers shown *below left* you will need:

Above, 2 pieces of olive wood, each 360 x 50 x 26mm (14 x 2 x 1in); carving gouges, 1/2in No 8 and 1/4in No 5; No 1 carving knife; oilstone; slip stone; light lubricating oil; leather strop; strop paste; walnut oil; soft cloth.

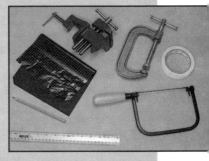

Above, carbon paper; masking tape; pencil; ruler; vice; G-clamp; coping saw and blade.

You have already learned how to do relief carving in wood in our fish and toucan projects. Now you can develop your skills further by working wood in the round — to make an attractive pair of salad servers — and we introduce you to the exciting and satisfying technique of whittling.

Carving decorative and utilitarian objects out of wood is an extremely ancient craft and a very satisfying one. The tools needed for woodcarving are fairly expensive, but if you have already done either of the earlier woodcarving projects you will already have the 1/4-inch and 1/2-inch gouges.

The main shapes of our salad servers are sawn from blocks of wood in two stages. First the bowl is cut — this allows you to use the gouge to carve the bowl while the block is held in the vice. The handle is then sawn and the final form is achieved by whittling the wood away with a knife.

We have used olive wood for our servers, but sycamore or maple would also be suitable. Olive is an attractive wood and is fairly easy to carve, but it has what is

known as a 'wild grain'. This means that the grain is not regular and runs in all directions throughout the wood. Very often the best way of cutting this sort of wood is across the grain, and this is where extra sharp tools will come into their own.

Whittle away

Whittling is one of the oldest and simplest carving techniques and is particularly associated with the folk carvings of the North American settlers. It lends itself to direct and spontaneous carvings — all you need are a block of wood, a very sharp knife and plenty of patience!

For all woodcarving, it is vital to have sharp tools, and to keep them sharp. Study the box on the next page which shows you how to strop your tools razor-sharp.

HELPFUL HINT

When whittling, always work away from your body and hand supporting the object so that if the carving knife slips, you are in no danger of cutting yourself. The implements used for whittling are extremely sharp and should be handled with caution.

133

TEMPLATES

Use templates A and B for the fork and the spoon, but leave out the prongs for the spoon. The dotted line indicates the depth to which the bowl is carved (step 7 and 8).

A

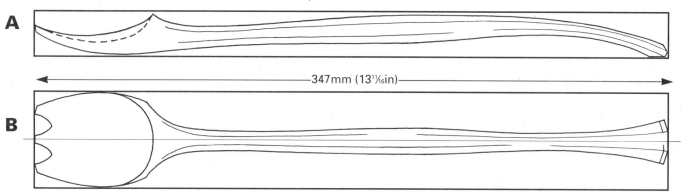

347mm (13¹¹⁄₁₆in)

B

SHARPENING AND STROPPING

Tools that are properly sharpened and stropped are mirror bright and cut smoothly and safely. They also have the ability to impart a polish to the cut surface of the wood.

A whittling knife is sharpened like a chisel (see the toucan carving project): hold the entire straight edge of the knife on the stone at about 15-20° to the surface, and rub it back and forth with some pressure to hone a bevel on one side. Turn it over and repeat on the other side. If you can look down on the edge in a good light and still see a silver line it is not sharp, so grind the blade again!

For fine and detailed carving, blades must be further sharpened by stropping. To strop the knife, place the leather strop on the table and put some strop paste on it. Lay the knife blade flat on the strop and pull it backwards several times, **1**. Repeat on the other side.

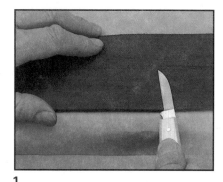

1

2

To strop a carving gouge, hold the strop as shown in the palm of one hand and pull the gouge towards you so that the bevel is in contact with the dressed leather, **2**. To strop the inside, bend the leather so that it fits the inside of the gouge and repeat the process, **3**.

Take particular care when handling your sharpened tools — they are dangerous. Protect the blades when the tools are not in use by keeping them covered with blade guards.

3

1 Enlarge the templates on a photocopier at 200% and cut around the rectangles. Cut pieces of carbon paper to the same size as these rectangles. Examine the wood carefully and if the pattern of the grain fits either the bowl of the server on the top surface, or the handle on the side of the wood, make use of it when positioning the template. Fix template A to a 26mm (1in)-wide side of a piece of wood

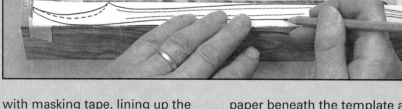

1

with masking tape, lining up the bottom of the bowl and the end of the handle with the bottom edge of the wood. Slip a piece of carbon

paper beneath the template and transfer the outline of the side of the server with a pencil. Remove the template and carbon paper.

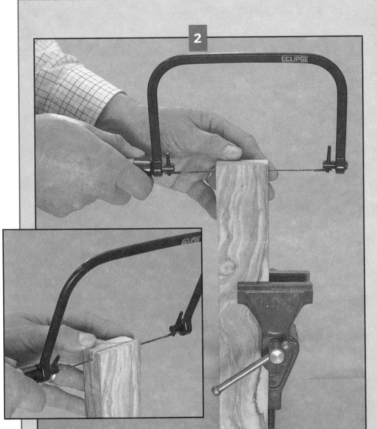

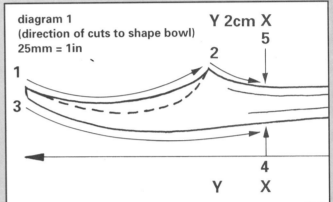

2 Secure the vice to the table and fix the wood as shown. With the blade of the coping saw parallel to the end of the wood, start making the first cut to shape the bowl (see diagram **1**). Saw slowly and squarely into the wood, keeping an eye on the profile you are cutting, and producing a smooth curve. Make the second cut, stopping about 2cm (³/₄in) from the peak of the bowl. Remove the saw and make the third cut on the underside of the bowl. Remove the saw, repositioning the wood in the vice for easy working if necessary, and make cuts 4 and 5 to remove the waste wood.

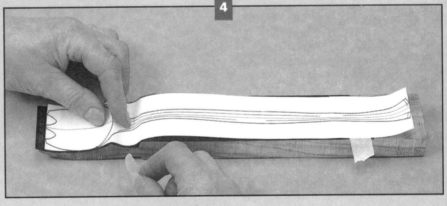

diagram 1
(direction of cuts to shape bowl)
25mm = 1in

Y 2cm X

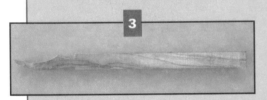

3 Remove the wood from the vice and check the profile.

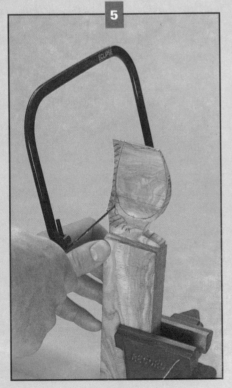

4 With a ruler and pencil, mark a central line along the top of the piece of wood. Position a piece of carbon paper and template B on this central line, matching point Y with the highest ridge of wood at the handle end of the bowl. Secure with masking tape. Transfer the outline of the 'shoulders' of the bowl to point X and all the outlines of the bowl except for the prongs. Move the template to the end of the bowl, join the outline freehand for a smooth line and draw in the prongs. Remove the template and carbon paper.

5 Fix the wood in the vice and, following diagram 2, saw away the sides of the bowl using three cuts on both sides.

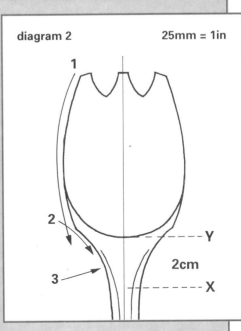

diagram 2   25mm = 1in

2cm

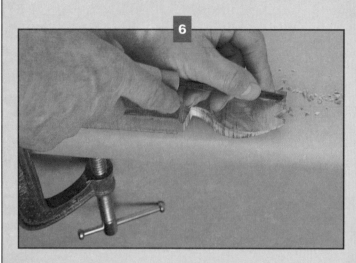

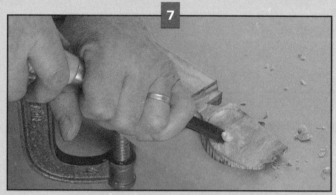

6 Clamp the wood to the table and carve away the V-shaped notches between the prongs. Holding the small gouge at about 45° and pushing with both hands, first make a tiny V, carving down to the centre of this area from both sides, then gradually carve out to the sides.

7 Using the No 8 gouge, carve away the wood from the inside of the bowl to a depth varying from 5mm (³/₁₆in) at the deepest point, to virtually nothing near the prongs (see template A, dotted line). Working round the bowl, carve from the sides to the centre of the bowl (see Helpful Hint).

8 Finish carving with small neat cuts for a 'tooled' finish.

HELPFUL HINT

When carving down into a concavity with the grain you will reach a point where the tool starts to cut against the grain and the hitherto smooth cut can become rough. The trick is to stop just before that point is reached and cut from the other side down to the same position from a different direction. Even so that crucial point where the grain turns from being with you to against you can be difficult to get smooth and this is where cutting across the grain can be helpful.

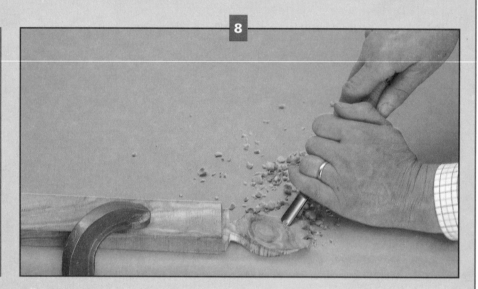

diagram 3   (direction of cuts to shape handle)

9 Using the lines drawn on the side of the wood in step 1, saw away the top and bottom profile of the handle with the coping saw (see diagram **3**), turning the wood in the vice as necessary. Make the small cuts to shape the end of the handle.

HELPFUL HINT

You will need to change the angle of the blade in the coping saw to allow you to clear the wood. Unscrew the handle to slacken the blade, and move the top and bottom peg to alter the blade to the required angle. Tighten up the handle, making sure that the two pegs are in line.

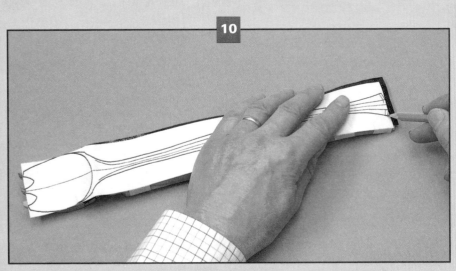

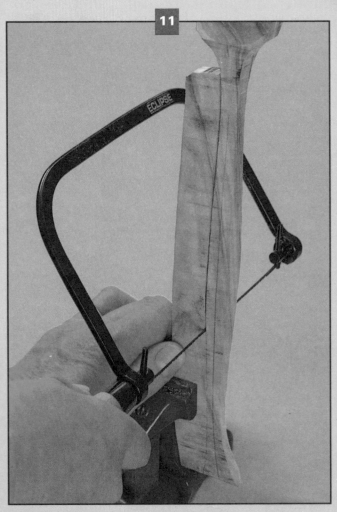

10 Draw in the central line on the top of the server if necessary and tape down template B, again positioning point Y to correspond with the high point on the bowl. Transfer all the lines for the handle through carbon paper on to the wood. The end of the template will fall short, so you must finish the drawing freehand, as shown.

11 Secure the wood in the vice and cut away both sides of the handle with the coping saw, again changing the angle of the blade.

HELPFUL HINT

You will have to note the way the grain runs as you carve all the curved surfaces and with olive wood sometimes the first indication you get that the grain has changed direction will be when the knife starts to dig in. For this reason take small cuts in one direction and be prepared to frequently change direction as the grain changes.

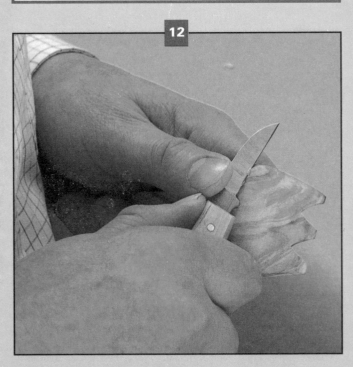

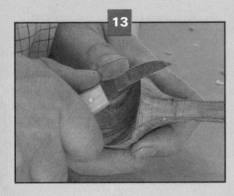

12 You can now start whittling with the knife. Make sure that the knife is razor sharp, and keep it sharp by stropping frequently. Start by cutting chips from the back of the bowl. Always cut with the grain, and cut away from yourself for safety. Use the thumb of the hand that is holding the wood as a guide.

13 Whittle the sides and the top of the bowl. Use the high points at the top and sides of the rear of the bowl as reference points. Carve up to these and, when you are satisfied that the shape is right, cut away the last remaining saw marks. Cut the ends of the two outside prongs at a slight angle.

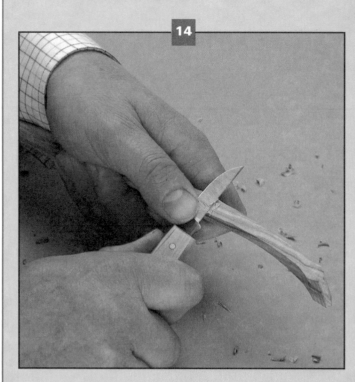

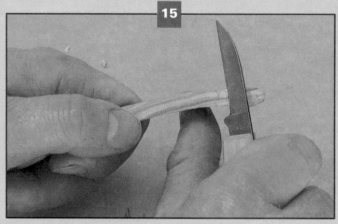

14 Now whittle the four sides of the handle, carving lightly with the knife to remove the saw marks and to achieve a smooth and pleasing outline.

15 When carving the sides of the end of the handle where it flares out you will have to pull the knife towards you to go with the grain so, for safety, keep your thumb beneath the handle while you do this.

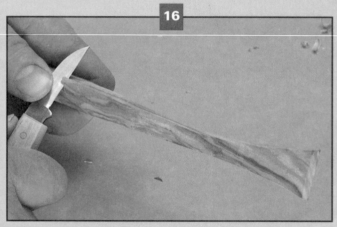

16 Now carve the four corners of the handle until you have achieved an octagonal profile (which will be comfortable to hold). Take the corners off the end of the handle to echo the shape of the outer prongs. Check the shape of the handle and of all the carving.

17 Make the spoon in the same way as the fork, but without the prongs. Apply several coats of walnut oil to the servers with a soft cloth, leaving each coat to dry before applying the next.

You can clean your salad servers by wiping them with a damp cloth after use (do not soak them in water). Treat them occasionally to a coat of walnut oil, which will deepen their colour, bring out the grain markings, and give them an attractive sheen.

SCULPTURE AND 3-D

RELIEF CARVING

To develop and refine your wood carving skills we show you in this project how to carve an endearing brown bear in low relief on a panel of limewood.

In a relief carving you are aiming to give an impression of the full three-dimensional form of the subject in a shallow space. So the rounded contours of the bear suggest that the form continues, and to imply distance, the furthest legs are reduced in height. The bear is carved in limewood, a hardwood that is easy to carve and takes detail well, but you could also use walnut or pearwood. A local timber merchants will probably cut you a piece to size.

If you have followed the previous three wood carving projects (the fish and the toucan carvings, and the salad servers) you will already have most of the equipment needed for this carving. In addition you will need a No 3 gouge (with a very shallow curve, nearly flat) and a No 10 gouge (with a nearly semi-circular profile), also known as a 'roughing out' gouge. Sharpen your tools before you begin carving, and strop them to keep them razor sharp as you work (see the toucan carving project for sharpening and the salad servers project for stropping).

Lustrous sheen

There is a wide variety of finishes that can be used on carvings, but a penetrating oil finish can often look better than any kind of varnish as the wood retains a natural look. We have used an oil treatment that only requires one application to achieve a fine lustrous sheen.

GRAIN OF THE WOOD

Wood cut to the size specified will generally have the grain running along its length. Cuts can be made in the direction of the grain, and across the grain; but if you get a rough finish when making a cut, this probably means you are cutting against the grain, and you should turn the piece round and cut in the opposite direction. The grain will vary in each piece of wood, so use the project as a guide to the order of cuts, but respond to your own piece of wood, moving it around as necessary.

We have specified particular tools for certain jobs, but as you become familiar with your tools you will want to make your own choices.

MATERIALS

To carve the bear shown *below left* you will need:

Above, limewood planed to a finished size of 320 x 235 x 20mm (12$^1/_2$ x 9$^1/_4$ x $^3/_4$in); sandpaper, coarse, medium & fine; cork block; 2 large G-clamps; 2 pieces of cork tile; masking tape; carbon paper; pencil.

Above, mallet; carving gouges, $^3/_8$in No 3, $^1/_4$in No 5, $^1/_2$in No 8, $^5/_{16}$in No 10; $^3/_{16}$in No 39 parting tool; No 1 carving knife; sharpening stone; slipstone; light lubricating oil; leather strop and strop paste.

Above, purified linseed oil; purified turpentine; jam jar with lid; saucepan; clean rags; hog's hair paint brush; wax furniture polish.

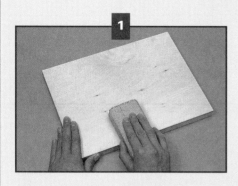

1 Smooth the surface of the wood with medium and then fine sandpaper, wrapping the sandpaper around a block of cork or wood to make a sanding block. Be careful not to use sandpaper that is too fine as this may burnish the wood rather than abrading it. Carefully brush and vacuum the wood after sanding to remove any pieces of abrasive material that will quickly blunt your gouges.

TEMPLATE

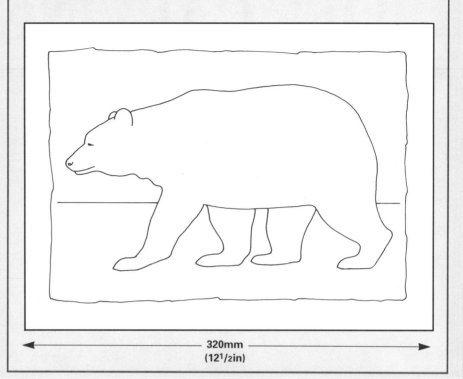

320mm
(12¹/₂in)

2 Enlarge the template on a photocopier at 200% and then again at 133%, and cut around the outer edge. Secure the template to the block of wood with masking tape and, using a piece of carbon paper, transfer the bear and border on to the wood with a pencil.

3 Remove the template and go over the line to strengthen it. Lightly draw lines on the border to indicate the position of the horizon line (which will be cut away).

4 Secure the edge of the wood to the work table with two G-clamps, protecting the wood with a scrap of cork tile. With the No 10 gouge and the mallet, cut a channel about 2mm (¹/₁₆in) from the outline of the border. Cut outside the outline of the bear in the same way, leaving the tight corners at the top of the legs.

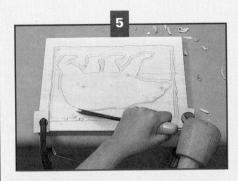

5 In some areas, such as the rear of the back, you will have to re-position the wood to carve the channel to avoid cutting against the grain.

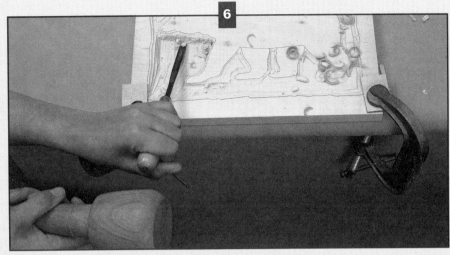

6 Using the No 10 gouge and the mallet, 'rough out' the background, starting at the border and working towards the bear as shown, working across the grain where possible to prevent the wood from splitting. Work carefully to get the depth correct. Refer to the diagram *below* as you cut further down into the wood. The shallowest area of the background near the feet will be about 6mm (¹⁄₄in) deep and the deepest (at the horizon line) about 12mm (¹⁄₂in).

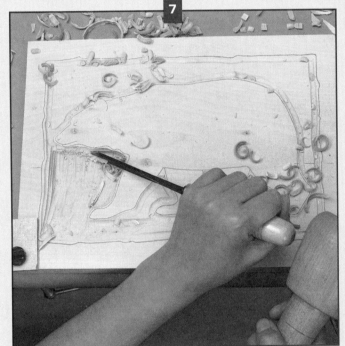

(all measurements in mm: 25mm = 1in)

10mm   back   12mm   left leg   right leg   6mm

belly   horizon

7 Cut away the wood left by the carving at the edge of the bear with a sideways cut as shown. Continue cutting away the background areas between the legs of the bear in the same way.

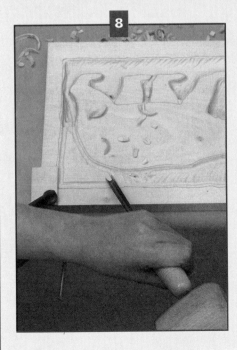

8 Re-position the wood and cut away the background from the top of the bear, changing the direction of the cuts when you begin to feel that you are working against the grain.

9 Cut away the areas between the legs using the gouge only (without the mallet) for more intricate areas. Continue to take down the background to the depth indicated in the diagram *above*.

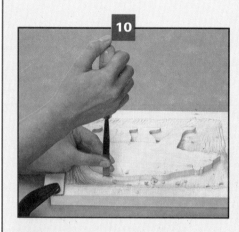

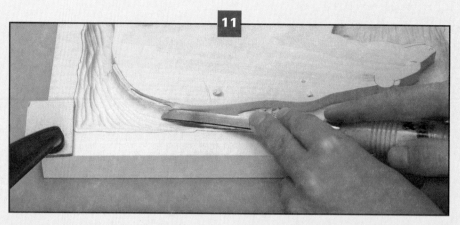

10 Cut down vertically around the outline of the bear to the full depth of the background. Use the No 3 gouge on the straighter parts of the outline, holding the blade quite near the wood and pushing with your hands, with the convex side of the gouge towards the bear as shown. When you cut down into the wood where the whole edge of the gouge is lying across the grain (at the rear of the bear), you may need to use the mallet to make the cuts. In areas with tighter curves, such as the paws, use smaller gouges, and hold them with the concave or convex side towards the bear as appropriate.

11 Holding the No 3 gouge at a shallow angle, slice away the chippings made by the vertical cuts. This will remove the waste wood and leave a well-defined edge around the bear. Do not remove any more of the background at this stage. It will be finished off after you have carved the bear.

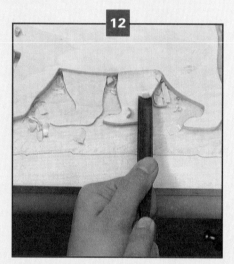

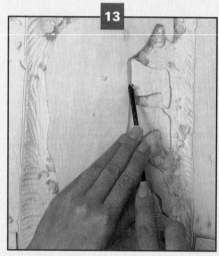

12 The two legs on the further side of the body are cut down to within 2mm (1/16in) of the background to give a sense of perspective. Start with a No 10 gouge to carve a channel (about 4mm (5/32in) deep) at the top of both legs. With the No 8 gouge, slice away the wood from the feet towards the belly as shown.

13 Use the parting tool to make a neat finish at the join between the legs and the body.

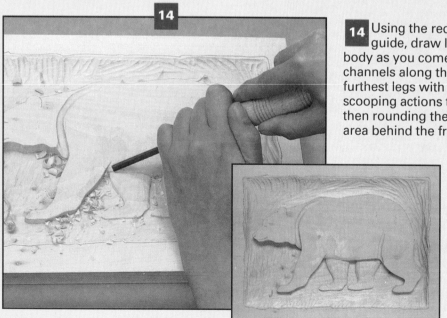

14 Using the red lines on the diagram *opposite* as a guide, draw lines to indicate the details of the body as you come to them. With a No 10 gouge, carve channels along these lines. Model the shape of the two furthest legs with the No 5 and 3 gouges, using small scooping actions to take off the sharp corners first, and then rounding the shape to model form. Shape the area behind the front leg and its join with the body.

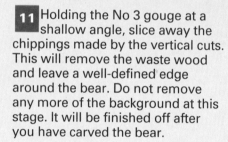

HELPFUL HINT

From step 14 it will be useful to refer to the final photograph of the bear carving in addition to the information in the steps. When carving the general shape of the bear use the No 3 gouge for the convex parts and the No 5 and 8 for the concave areas.